THE
BIBLE FOR
GROWN-UPS

A NEW LOOK AT
THE GOOD BOOK

Simon Loveday

ICON

This edition published in the UK in 2017
by Icon Books Ltd, Omnibus Business Centre,
39–41 North Road, London N7 9DP
email: info@iconbooks.com
www.iconbooks.com

First published in the UK in 2016 by Icon Books Ltd

Sold in the UK, Europe and Asia
by Faber & Faber Ltd, Bloomsbury House,
74–77 Great Russell Street,
London WC1B 3DA or their agents

Distributed in the UK, Europe and Asia
by Grantham Book Services,
Trent Road, Grantham NG31 7XQ

Distributed in the USA by Publishers Group West,
1700 Fourth Street, Berkeley, CA 94710

Distributed in Canada by Publishers Group Canada,
76 Stafford Street, Unit 300, Toronto, Ontario M6J 2S1

Distributed in Australia and New Zealand
by Allen & Unwin Pty Ltd, PO Box 8500,
83 Alexander Street, Crows Nest, NSW 2065

Distributed in South Africa
by Jonathan Ball, Office B4, The District,
41 Sir Lowry Road, Woodstock 7925

Distributed in India by Penguin Books India,
7th Floor, Infinity Tower – C, DLF Cyber City,
Gurgaon 122002, Haryana

ISBN: 978-178578-263-3

Typeset in Bembo by Marie Doherty

Printed and bound in the UK by Clays Ltd, St Ives plc

THE
BIBLE FOR
GROWN-UPS

CONTENTS

LIST OF ILLUSTRATIONS

ABOUT THE AUTHOR

Simon Loveday trained as an anthropologist and a literary critic, teaching at UEA and Oxford. He also edited the psychological journal *Typeface* and wrote *The Romances of John Fowles*. He lectured at Keele University and lived in Wells, Somerset, where he was at one time Chair of the Wells Festival of Literature. Simon Loveday died in October 2016.

For Sheena

PERMISSIONS

I should like to thank the following for permission to use copyright material:

Bloomsbury Publishing Inc., for material from *Awkward Reverence: Reading the New Testament Today*, by Paul Q. Beeching

Faber & Faber, and New Directions Publishing, for material from 'The Airy Christ', by Stevie Smith

Penguin Random House LLC, for material from *Zealot: The Life and Times of Jesus of Nazareth*, by Reza Aslan

Victoria University in the University of Toronto, for material from *The Great Code: The Bible and Literature*, by H. Northrop Frye

ACKNOWLEDGEMENTS

At various stages during the writing of this book I have been enormously helped by encouragement, advice, and detailed (but always constructive!) criticism, from a number of people, including Stuart Andrews, Roger Ashley, Michael Cansdale, James John, Gareth Jones, William Keyser, Bill White, and my editor at Icon, Duncan Heath. Tim Wood, of St Andrews Press, Kate Noble, and Chris Lee have kindly helped me with diagrams and design. All errors are of course my own responsibility.

PROLOGUE

'When I was a child, I spake as a child, I understood
as a child, I thought as a child; but when I
became a man, I put away childish things.'

(1 Corinthians 13:11)*

If you are a regular listener to BBC Radio 4, you cannot
have avoided *Desert Island Discs*. A famous personality is ship-
wrecked on an imaginary island and asked to choose their
eight favourite records. At the end they are offered one luxury
and one book – *in addition to the Bible and Shakespeare*.

Desert Island Discs is not a religious programme, nor are its
guests chosen for their religious beliefs. Yet the formula has
not changed in over 50 years. Two books are felt to need no
justification. One is by an author universally acknowledged to
be among the greatest dramatists and poets who ever lived. But
the other is ... well, what is it exactly? Is it a work of faith?
Then what use is it to atheists, or to believers in a different

---

* All quotations are from the Authorised Version, the King James
Bible. Where newer Bible translations are more accurate, I have
shown the amendments in square brackets.

faith? Is it a work of philosophy, a guide to life? If so, what is the philosophy it puts forward? What are we to make of its frequent condemnation of non-believers? Is it Christian – or Jewish? Is it a set of beliefs? A framework of moral rules? Or just a collection of stories and poems?

Every Christmas, small children write their letters to Santa Claus to tell him what they specially want. As they grow up, children progressively lose their belief in Santa: we might be sorry to meet a four-year-old who did not believe in him, but we would be more troubled by a fourteen-year-old (or a 40-year-old) who did. There is a childish way of thinking about Santa – and there is Santa for grown-ups.

Every Christmas, the same small children in Western schools are carefully coached to act out the story of a child announced by an angel, fathered by a spirit, pointed out by a star, and born to a virgin. None of this – and very little of what surrounds it in the Bible – corresponds to our everyday reality any more than the story of Santa Claus: most of it, indeed, considerably less. Yet no one tells us how to make the transition from the innocent belief of the child, to a mature ability to get these stories into perspective.

There is a childish way of thinking about the Bible – but what is an adult way? What, in short, would be 'the Bible for grown-ups'?

The intention of this book is not to break new ground, nor to be contentious. There is a huge amount of careful, thoughtful, and fascinating Biblical research and scholarship from the past two centuries; but all too often it does not get over the academic frontier. This book seeks to make that research more widely known, in terms that the general reader can understand.

The book is theologically neutral. It neither requires, nor rejects, belief. What it tries to do is to help intelligent adults to make sense of the Bible – a book that is too large to swallow whole, yet too important in our history and culture to spit out. How do we approach the Bible, not with the naivete of the child, but with the maturity of the adult? How can we read the Bible with our brains in gear? The purpose of this book is to do just that.

PART ONE

THE OLD TESTAMENT

1. The structure of the Bible

The groundwork for this chapter was laid in 2011 – the 400th anniversary of the publication of the King James Bible. The radio was full of praise for the beautiful prose and the magical rhythm of that 1611 translation, which has become not only a flagship and standard-bearer for the English language, but also the best-selling book in history. The words of the King James Bible are woven into the lives, and the hearts, of many of us who went to Church schools, grew up with Anglican services, and sang its psalms. Weddings bring us its message of love, funerals its words of consolation and hope. But there is a remarkable omission from all this celebration. The King James Bible is not an original work – it is a translation. What is it a translation of? What was the original, and how did it come into existence?

The Bible as we now have it consists of three parts: the Old Testament, the Apocrypha, and the New Testament. ('Testament' here means a kind of contract; the Old Testament defined one kind of contract between God and man, the New Testament redefined that contract.)

The Old Testament – known to modern Jews as the Hebrew Bible – consists of about 39 books. (Catholics and Protestants recognise 39; other Christian denominations, such as Ethiopian and Coptic, recognise up to four more.) These were written down in Hebrew or Aramaic between about 900 BC (or possibly later) and about 160 BC. They were then translated into

Greek and became widely available – to Jews and Gentiles – around the Mediterranean. The core of the Bible is usually regarded as the first eleven books (from Genesis through Kings, omitting Ruth). These books tell a continuous story and take the Israelites from the creation of the world through to the fall of Jerusalem in 587 BC. For the Old Testament part of this book, it is the first part of this core – the five books known as the Pentateuch – that I will focus on.

The Apocrypha (from the Greek for 'that which is hidden away') consists of about sixteen books – again, different branches of Christianity vary in their precise selection – mostly composed in late pre-Christian times. The Roman Catholic Church accepts it as a part of the Old Testament and so of the Bible, but the Anglican Church does not. It does not have the same 'canonical' status as the other parts of the Bible, and consequently, though it is very stimulating (it contains, for example, the world's first detective stories), I will not be discussing it in this book.

The New Testament consists of 27 books – the four Gospels, the Acts of the Apostles, the Letters (or Epistles) of St Paul and others, and the Revelation of St John. It tells the story of Jesus and his followers from the birth of Jesus (somewhere between 6 and 4 BC), through his death around 30–35 AD, till shortly after the fall of Jerusalem in 70 AD. It was written in Greek between about 43 AD and about 120 AD, but did not take final form until the 4th century AD.

An obvious point that is often missed is that both the Old and the New Testament were written by Jews (with the possible exception of Mark and Luke), about Jews, and largely for Jews; virtually every major character in both books, from Abel to Zebedee, from the patriarchs to the prophets, and from Adam to Jesus, is Jewish. Given the long history of Christian anti-Semitism round the world, that is quite a sobering thought!

2. The authority of the Bible[1]

> 'Ye shall not add unto the word which I command you, neither shall ye diminish aught from it ... what thing soever I command you, observe to do it'
>
> (Deuteronomy 4:2 and 12:32)

Christianity is a world religion: at the last count there were almost a thousand million Christians scattered round the globe. There is a huge diversity under the Christian umbrella, but we can confidently expect every Christian to share at least two beliefs: one, that there was a special person called Jesus who lived and died in Palestine 2,000 years ago and who sets an example that Christians must follow; and two, that there was and is a special book, the Bible, that has a particular authority and claim to truth for all Christians and indeed for all humanity.

The authority of the Bible is not just a matter for abstruse theological debate. The question whether justification should be by faith or by works – argued with reference not only to the New Testament, but also to God's promise to Abraham in Genesis 15:1–6 – was a major factor underlying Martin Luther's departure from the Catholic Church in 1521; religious wars raged throughout Europe in the 16th and 17th centuries over the question of whether or not Christ was present in the bread and water of the host (Matthew 26:26–28); millions of individual fates to this day have been determined by the restrictions on divorce, and on the remarriage of divorcees, drawn from Jesus' remarks in Matthew 19:3–9; and the restrictions on 'usury' (lending money at interest) drawn from Leviticus 25:36–37 governed the financial life of Europe throughout the late Middle Ages.

These are not just historical influences. Nor are they confined to Christians – for Muslims, Jews and Christians all draw on a common body of Old Testament stories and characters, recognise Jesus as a historical figure, and describe themselves as 'people of the book'. Homosexual behaviour, notably between men, is banned in many parts of the world by reference to Leviticus 20:13; drawing on Old Testament principles, the Qur'an forbids the payment of interest and has consequently given rise to 'Islamic banking' throughout the Arab world; and the boundaries of the Promised Land set out in Joshua are used by the modern state of Israel to determine settlement policy in Jordan and the West Bank. Even more striking in its focus on a single Biblical text is the continuing decision of the Catholic Church to reject contraception on the grounds that Onan displeased God because he 'spilled [his seed] on the ground' (Genesis 38:9).

Reference to Catholicism may make Protestants feel a little smug. This would be unwise. Catholics believe that the authority of Scripture is interpreted by the 'magisterium' of the Church: as a result there is a continuing process of re-interpretation of doctrine going on within the Catholic Church, expressed in a series of Papal encyclicals. Recent examples are the increasing attention and status given to women in the Catholic Church (for example, the doctrine of the perpetual virginity of Mary, the mother of Jesus) and the way in which Catholics have reformed their attitude to and teaching on Jews. In these matters the Catholics are ahead of the Bible, which says nothing about Mary's perpetual virginity (especially given that Jesus has a number of brothers and sisters (Matthew 13:55 and Mark 6:3)) and robustly blames Jews for the Crucifixion (Matthew 27:25, Mark 15:12–14, Luke 23:13–24, John 19:14–16).

By contrast, Protestantism arose as a rebellion against the way the Church stood between man and God; it has rested from the start on a conviction that men and women need no priests to interpret the word of God, and that all answers are to be found in the Bible. William Tyndale, who in the 1520s wrote the first translation of the Bible into English, remarked angrily to a fellow clergyman that 'if God spares my life, ere many years I will cause the boy that driveth the plow to know more of the Scriptures than thou dost!' Protestants depend on the authority of Scripture because there isn't any higher authority to appeal to.

3. The historical context: the world in which the Old Testament took shape

The chorus of praise for the King James Bible often seems to suggest that the book was written in 1611 (and in English). But it was not.* The Hebrew Bible that we know as the Old Testament was not the product of one mind, nor was it the product of one time or even of one country (much of the Old Testament was written in Babylon, and the bulk of the New Testament was certainly written outside Palestine). There are four points of critical importance for an understanding of this element of the Bible:

a) the Old Testament is the work of a variety of authors over several hundred years;

b) every word of the Old Testament has been copied and re-copied, written and re-written, edited and re-edited, many times on the way to its present form (for English-speaking readers, we must add translated and re-translated);

c) Old Testament authors wrote within a social and political context, and with their own social and political purposes – which frequently included the fervent wish to take issue with another Old Testament author. The work cannot be understood without some knowledge of this background;

* 'That the Bible was not written originally in English is a fact not always appreciated, and there are even now those who are unaware of it' – *New Oxford Annotated Bible*, OUP, 1991.

d)   paradoxically, we know more about those who wrote the Old Testament than we do about those who wrote the New Testament.

To start to understand the Old Testament, let's begin by considering the world in which it unfolds. We have seen that its books were first written down between about 900 BC and about 160 BC. Some of the happenings described in the text (e.g. the events that take place in Egypt and are described in Genesis and Exodus) are presented as having happened some hundreds of years earlier; a few (the creation of the world described in Genesis, the Flood, the covenant with Abraham) are placed even earlier. But the majority of the events of the Bible are presented as having taken place in the first millennium BC.

To put that in context, Diagram 1 shows what was happening around the Mediterranean during that period.

By 3000 BC, Egypt was a functioning kingdom, the first Pyramids were being built, and writing was being used to record both sacred and secular information. There was a highly developed knowledge of mathematics for surveying, irrigation, and astronomy, a meticulous bureaucratic system of records, and a professional class of scribes to control the religious activities of the people of Egypt. There were long-standing trading relationships with countries throughout Africa and as far north as Britain (where the first circular ditch was just being dug at Stonehenge). Further to the east, in Sumeria, the Law Code of King Urukagina embodied rules of social justice, and the

	3500 BC onwards	2000 BC onwards	1000 BC onwards
Egypt	High kingdom under Pharaohs. Pyramids built. Writing, mathematics, professional scribes. Trading across Europe and Africa, dominant power in Near East.		Becomes weaker and eventually falls to Persians and then to Greeks.
Babylon, Sumeria, Assyria	Rising city states. Law code of Sumerian King Urukagina, 2350 BC: 'The rich should not oppress the poor; widows and orphans do not pay tax.' Sumerian *Epic of Gilgamesh* includes flood myth.	Fall of Sumeria. Babylon and Assyria become warring empires. Law codes. (Babylonian Code of Hammurabi, 1750 BC: 'An eye for an eye, a tooth for a tooth.')	Babylon and Assyria dominant powers in the region. Finally fall to Persian Empire by 536 BC.
Israel (northern kingdom of the Israelites, capital Samaria)		First mentioned in Egyptian records c. 1200 BC as part of Egypt.	Supposed kingdom of David and Solomon, c. 1000 BC; splits into northern and southern kingdoms before 900 BC. / 722 BC, northern kingdom of Israel overrun and erased by Assyrians, resettled with Gentiles, becomes Samaria.
Judah (southern kingdom of the Israelites, capital Jerusalem)			587 BC, southern kingdom of Judah conquered by Babylonians, Temple destroyed, king and priests exiled.
Hebrew Bible			Earliest written Bible stories from about 900 BC. / Ten Commandments written down c. 700–450 BC.

Diagram 1. Writing, law, and power in the ancient world.

Epic of Gilgamesh set out a creation myth and a flood myth with strong parallels in the much later book of Genesis.

By 2000 BC, writing was widespread round the Mediterranean. Sumeria had fallen, but the kingdoms of Babylon and Assyria were rising to power and competing with each other. A number of legal systems had been set out in written form, including the famous phrase, 'an eye for an eye and a tooth for a tooth' (from the Babylonian Code of Hammurabi).

By 1000 BC, the moment at which the Bible stories start to intersect with events that can be authenticated from other written material, the Egyptian Empire was in decline, but other powers were on the rise (Assyria, Babylon, and Persia). The Greeks were beginning to expand across the Mediterranean (the Philistines, mentioned frequently in the Bible, are thought to be a Greek offshoot). The Minoan civilisation of Knossos had risen and fallen, probably because of the explosion of the volcanic island of Santorini around 1450 BC. Ugaritic (Canaanite) epics such as *The Palace of Ba'al* had appeared in writing and are thought to have influenced much later Biblical writings (Deuteronomy 32:7–9). And by 900 BC the Israelites* themselves were living in two kingdoms – Israel in the north, with its capital first at Samaria and then

---

* It is not easy to find the right terminology to refer to the people who are now thought of as the forebears of the modern Jews. For simplicity I shall refer to them as Israelites or the people of Israel in the Old Testament and Jews in the New, with apologies for the considerable over-simplification this involves.

at Shechem, and Judah or Judea, with its capital Jerusalem, in the south – which pretty closely overlap the modern country of Israel.

The Bible relates that those kingdoms were united around that time by the most famous Israelite king, King David, whose reign the Bible dates to about 1000–962 BC. The Old Testament books of Samuel, Kings, and Chronicles tell us that between 1000 and 800 BC, the kingdoms of Israel and Judah – united under David and his son Solomon, then divided by civil war under Solomon's sons Rehoboam and Jeroboam, but always aware of a common language and a common religion – flourished both militarily and economically. The Bible recounts that the First Temple was built by Solomon with great magnificence; that alliances were established, many through marriage (Solomon was reputed to have 700 wives, creating in the process 700 political connections with other tribes and states); that trade expanded widely; that a professional army was built up, replacing the old tribal levies; that a network of cities developed; and that power was centralised in Jerusalem, capital of the southern kingdom of Judah.

However, this was also the period of growth of two mighty empires further east, in Mesopotamia: Babylon and Assyria. Israel and Judah were more powerful than their immediate neighbours and had overcome the small kingdoms of Moab and Edom to the east. But they were far out of their depth against the superpowers.

In 722 BC, after a series of attacks, we know from historical and archaeological evidence that the Assyrians conquered

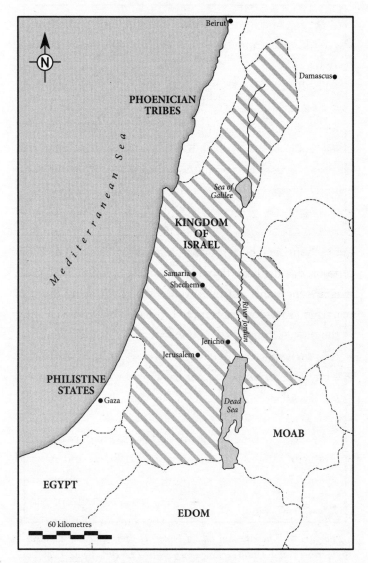

Diagram 2. The rise and fall of Israel, I. The kingdom united under Solomon (c. 950 BC).

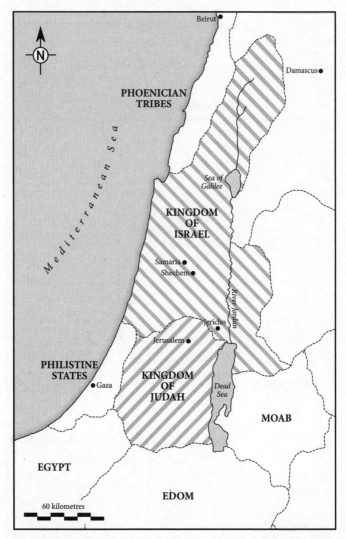

Diagram 3. The rise and fall of Israel, II. The kingdom divided:
the northern and southern kingdoms, 900–722 BC. J and E authors
begin Genesis, Exodus, Numbers. Hosea, Amos, Micah, Isaiah
create prophetic books.

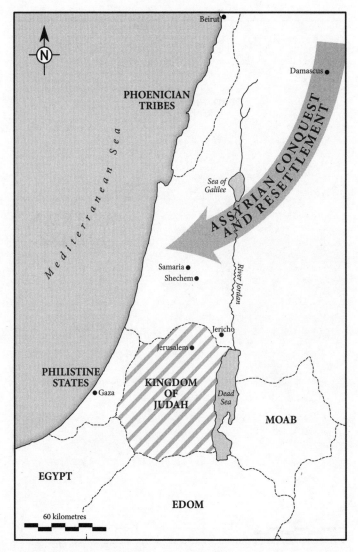

Diagram 4. The rise and fall of Israel, III. The fall of the northern kingdom, 722–587 BC. The Priestly elements of Genesis, Exodus, Numbers. Jeremiah writes 'Deuteronomist history'.

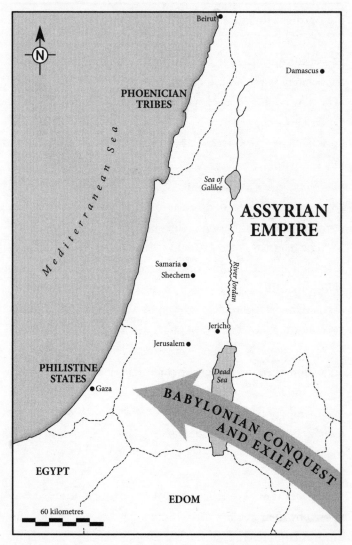

Diagram 5. The rise and fall of Israel, IV. The Babylonian conquest and exile, 587–536 BC. (Massive writing, collating, editing takes place in Babylonian exile.)

the northern kingdom of Israel, plundered its cities, enslaved many of its citizens, and resettled the land with a variety of peoples from different parts of their empire, in the process deliberately wiping out the pure worship of the God of Israel. (The new country became known as Samaria, and its people as Samaritans – the very same as we meet in the New Testament parable.) The refugees fled south to Judah. In the process they brought with them their version of the religion of their people, their versions of the sacred stories, and a heightened focus on what separated both the northern and the southern peoples from the different religious and national groups in the region.

The religious systems around the Mediterranean overlapped to a high degree: from Babylon across to Greece, and from before 1000 BC right through to the Christian era, Ashtaroth (or Ishtar, or Aphrodite, or Venus) was the high goddess, Marduk (or El, or Zeus, or Jupiter) was the chief of the council of the gods, and there were constellations of lesser gods performing specific functions within the greater whole. More importantly still, the gods were relaxed about pluralism as long as the order of precedence was respected: when a country conquered another or forced it into a vassal role, images of the conqueror's gods would be installed in the temples of the subject people to represent their control over their subjects.

By contrast, even at this early stage the Israelites were known by their neighbours as distinctively monotheistic. This was not completely true yet: the Elephantine Temple, set up by an Israelite community in Egypt in the 8th century BC, contained statues to a number of gods, and it may be more accurate to call the Israelites at that stage henotheistic (that is, believing that many gods exist, but their own god is superior). There are many traces of this belief in the Old Testament, and the constant tirades by the prophets against the worship of idols make it clear that the ordinary people of Israel displayed a regrettable tendency to spread their bets among a number of gods. However, within the territory of Israel and Judah, there was no room, officially at least, for any god but God.

The fall of the northern kingdom of Israel in 722 BC was followed by the decline of Judah, the southern kingdom, as it became squeezed between Egypt on one side and the rising power of Babylon on the other. In 609 BC King Josiah was killed fighting against the Egyptians; in the next twenty years Judah was successively the vassal of Egypt and Babylon; and in 587 BC the unthinkable happened. After an unsuccessful rebellion, King Zedekiah was defeated by the forces of Babylon and forced to watch the execution of both his sons, after which he was blinded. Jerusalem was sacked, the Temple was destroyed, thousands of Jews were deported to Babylon, and many of the survivors fled – taking refuge, by a cruel irony, in the land of their old oppressor, Egypt. God's chosen people no longer had a home.

4. The structure and purpose of the Old Testament: the mission statement for the Israelites

'Now the Lord had said unto Abram, "Get thee out of thy country, and from thy kindred, and from thy father's house, unto a land that I will shew thee; And I will make of thee a great nation, and I will bless thee, and make thy name great; and thou shalt be a blessing: And I will bless them that bless thee, and curse him that curseth thee: and in thee shall all families of the earth be blessed".'

(Genesis 12:1–3)

'Behold, I set before you this day a blessing and a curse; A blessing, if ye obey the commandments of the Lord your God, which I command thee this day: And a curse, if ye will not obey the commandments of the Lord your God, but turn aside out of the way which I command you this day, to go after other gods, which ye have not known.'

(Deuteronomy 11:26–28)

The Old Testament, or Hebrew Bible – 'Bible' being a translation of the Greek 'ta biblia', 'the little books' or 'the scrolls' – was written down well before the birth of Christ, and makes up well over half the Bible: and the Old Testament is not Christian. It was not only written *by* Israelites. It was also written *for* Israelites. *In fact it is the mission statement for the Israelites*: the assertion that they are the people chosen by God not only to be the moral compass to the world, but also to rule over it.

So what is in the Old Testament? The 39 books can be grouped into four categories, and we can sum them up as follows.

First are the five books known to Greeks as the Pentateuch, and to Jews as the Torah (often translated as 'laws', but better rendered as 'instruction'). These books – Genesis, Exodus, Leviticus, Numbers, and Deuteronomy – tell the story of the people of Israel from the creation of the world, the Flood, the covenant with Abraham, the exile in Egypt, the escape from Pharaoh, the crossing of the Red Sea, and the 40 years in the wilderness. They end when Moses, having led his people through the wilderness of Sinai, dies on the very border of the Promised Land of Israel.

Included seamlessly in this narrative sweep is a mass of law-giving of which the most famous element – repeated, with variations, on three different occasions – is the Ten Commandments.

This first part of the Old Testament tells the story of 'how we gained the kingdom': how the Israelites returned to the land that they believed God had given them, and the moral and ritual principles that were to govern their lives in that land.

The second group of books – Joshua, Judges, 1 and 2 Samuel, 1 and 2 Kings, 1 and 2 Chronicles – are known as the Histories. These books – which are written in the style and form of history rather than of myth – feature such celebrated figures as Saul, David, and Solomon, and tell the story of the life of the Israelites in their newly conquered kingdom, from rule by judges to rule by kings, from unity to division, and finally to the fall of Jerusalem in 587 BC and the exile in Babylon. Put simply, it is 'how we lost the kingdom'.

The third group is the Prophets. If the first two are 'what happened', this group of writers ask 'why it happened' – why things went wrong, and what the Israelites should do about it. Most of the prophecies were written at roughly the same time as the Histories, but are kept distinct from them (unlike the unashamed mixing of genres in the Torah) because they are of a different genre – much as modern newspapers seek, not always successfully, to separate news from comment. These are emphatically comment (and seldom news). The prophets – Amos, Hosea, Isaiah, Jeremiah, Micah, Jonah, and many others – consider the former greatness and present humiliation of Israel, explaining it as God's punishment for the way the Israelites disobeyed the divine instructions. There is no falling away from the sense of a mission conferred on the Israelites by God: defeat simply strengthens the urgency of the need to understand the divine plan, and put things right.

Finally there are about a dozen books that do not fall into any of the three categories above. Some continue the historical account (Ezra, Nehemiah) in the world of exile and return; some are philosophical meditations on life (Job, Proverbs, Ecclesiastes); there are religious and secular poems (Psalms, the Song of Solomon), and romantic tales (Esther, Ruth). Some of these are highly charged with religion; some (Ecclesiastes) explicitly deny that religion can explain anything. In the Hebrew Bible these books are simply grouped as 'Writings', which is as good a way of describing them as any other.

The date at which the Old Testament books were written bears no relation to their place in the sequence. Much of Genesis, which opens the Bible, was written after 700 BC, but prophets such as Hosea and Amos (respectively numbers 28 and 30 of the 39 books) wrote almost a century earlier, while the *Oxford Bible Commentary* dates the earliest element of the entire Old Testament, the triumph song of Deborah and Barak (Judges Chapter 5 – the seventh book of the Bible), to the 12th century BC, over 300 years before Genesis was begun. The sequence of 39 books that we have now (see Appendix 1) is the result of very careful editorial (re)arrangement.*

Finally, we should note that the Old Testament contains a full spread of genres and styles: sacred and secular, laws and philosophy, geography and genealogy, songs of praise and songs of love. As the *Oxford Bible Commentary* puts it, 'we cannot assume that the writers saw any distinction between "sacred" and "secular" history'.

* The Old Testament as we have it now, Part One of the sacred book of the Christians, is as we have seen almost identical to the Hebrew Bible, the sacred book of the Jewish people. The order of the books in the Hebrew Bible is somewhat different, and there are some differences as to which books are included, but for the most part the early Christian Church simply took over the Jewish scriptures. In fact there are more differences between Christian faiths as to what should go into the Old Testament, than between Christianity and Judaism (Protestants, Catholics, Orthodox, and Ethiopian Christians all have a different set of books in their Old Testament canon).

5. The Old Testament as history: what story does the Old Testament tell? And is it true?

The Bible begins with three great stories: the creation of Adam and Eve, the expulsion from Eden, and the great flood (Genesis 1–9). These stories, which refer to the whole of humanity rather than only to the people of Israel, are often (though not universally) regarded as mythical rather than historical truths, and I will not elaborate on them here. But they quickly give way to stories that do lay claim to historical truth; stories, not of the birth of man, but of the birth of the Israelites.

Genesis recounts that the people of Israel did not originate in Israel. It says that they came originally from the land of the Sumerians (modern-day Iraq – Genesis 10:10), and travelled to Canaan (modern Palestine) and thence to Egypt (Exodus Chapter 1), where they were enslaved. From there, by the direct intervention of God and under the leadership of the prophet Moses, they were released and after 40 years in the wilderness, returned to the Promised Land, the modern Israel (Exodus through Deuteronomy). This they invaded, putting its occupants to the sword and dividing the land among themselves (Joshua).

The liberation of the Israelites from servitude and captivity in Egypt has an importance in the Jewish, Israeli, and indeed the world imagination that it would be hard to over-estimate. The very word 'exodus' is instantly meaningful to people for whom the Bible is literally a closed book; the image of a suffering people released from slavery and guided to safety by a protective God resonates with us all. And it is usually taught, both in Christian religious groups and in modern Israeli schools, as a historical truth.

To fit it in with the chronology of Saul, David, and Solomon (around 1020–920 BC), the events of the Pentateuch are usually posited to have happened over the preceding thousand years: Abraham's journey from Ur to Canaan about 2000 or 1900 BC, the descent into Egypt shortly after that, and the Exodus – after 400 years in Egypt – in the 13th century BC. But powerful, even universal, though this story is, we have to say that outside the Bible itself there is not a single shred of historical evidence to support it. Indeed recent historical scholarship actually undermines it even further.

To take a specific point: the Genesis stories of Abraham, Isaac, and Jacob – which the sequence of events in the Old Testament places around the 19th or 20th century BC – make frequent references to Philistines and Aramaeans. These peoples are well authenticated in the archaeological and the historical record – but not until the 12th century BC at the very earliest, and in the case of the Aramaeans, not reaching the height of their powers till the 9th century BC, a thousand years after their appearance in the Bible story. (To give a modern parallel, it is as if we spoke of the role of the Vikings in the fight against Hitler.)

The same difficulty recurs with camels. These are frequently cited in Genesis (for example, 12:16, 24 passim, 30:43) and Exodus (9:3). Unfortunately the historical and archaeological evidence admits of no doubt: camels were not domesticated until 1000 BC at the earliest, a thousand years too late.

But there are more powerful objections. The Egyptian state meticulously documented the events of the reign of each Pharaoh. Though there are records of nomadic peoples in Egypt, there is no record of the 400-year presence of a Hebrew people there; there is no record of a persecution of such a people; there is no record of a rebellion, or an exodus. Moreover the Biblical date for such an exodus – around the 13th century BC – throws up a further problem: at that time Palestine was an Egyptian province. The escape would have been out of Egypt, into … Egypt. The Bible story of 600,000 warriors, together with wives and children – a group of at least two million – travelling through a barren desert, is not merely improbable: it is supposed to have happened in a period well documented in Egyptian records, and it left in those records no trace whatsoever. The Biblical Mount Sinai from which Moses descended with the Ten Commandments has never been found, and settlements mentioned in the narrative – Pithom, Etzion-Gever, Arad – did not exist until centuries later. The rise of Biblical archaeology in the second half of the 20th century was expected to produce the evidence that is lacking from the historical record, but it has become painfully clear – painfully to many of those who sought such evidence – that it is simply not there.[2] The first reference to 'Israelites' occurs on an Egyptian stone tablet dated around 1200 BC, but it places them already in Palestine. We have seen that Egyptian records make no mention of them in the Egypt of the time.

The next key event in the history of the Israelites is the capture of the Promised Land by Joshua: 'Moses my servant is dead; now therefore arise, go over this Jordan, thou, and all this people, unto the land which I give to them, even to the children of Israel. Every place that the sole of your foot shall tread upon, that have I given unto you, as I said unto Moses. From the wilderness and this Lebanon even unto the great river, the river Euphrates, all the land of the Hittites, and unto the great sea toward the going down of the sun, shall be your coast' (Joshua 1:2–4). The bloody battles for that promised land – the defeat of Jericho and the massacre of all its inhabitants including women, children, and animals (Joshua 6:21), the conquest of Ai and the death of the 12,000 male and female inhabitants (Joshua 8:25–26), the massacre of every living thing in the conquered settlements (Joshua 11:11–14), and the overthrow of the 31 kings of that country (Joshua 12:7–24) – are followed by a careful division and allocation of the land between the twelve tribes of Israel and a rigorous instruction not to intermarry with the survivors of the ethnic cleansing (Joshua 23:12–13). Israel has come into its own: the Promised Land has been won.

Alas, this story, like the exodus that preceded it, finds no support whatever from the archaeological record. There is no evidence of a change of culture in the Palestine of the time; no record of mighty battles or of slaughter beyond the general run of small wars that were universal in the late Bronze Age; no sign of a decisive shift of peoples or movement of armies. Many historians (though with no support from the archaeological record) take a political rather than a religious view of the conquest of Israel, seeing it as a revolt by the Israelite peasants against their rulers; but whatever the theories, there is no support in history for the story in the Bible. Perhaps the Israelites were just one of the many tribal groups – Ammonites, Canaanites, Midianites, Hivites, Jebusites, Moabites, Perizzites – who lived in Palestine at that time. We simply don't know. 'The book of Joshua tells a powerful tale of conquest, supported by a God who showed no respect for most of the Holy Land's existing inhabitants. Even now, the tale has not lost its power, but it is not history and it never was.'[3]

At this point the reader may be thinking that it is no great achievement to punch holes in the 'mythical' early part of the Bible: after all, most Christians no longer accept the literal truth of the Creation story, so why should they expect literal truth from the Exodus narrative? Most Bible readers probably feel – as I did – that when we get on to the 'Histories' in Samuel, Kings, and Chronicles (the part of the Old Testament that recounts the rise of Jerusalem and the political unification of the kingdom under Saul, David, and Solomon), we are onto solid historical ground. The style of the writing changes, the reference to historical places becomes more secure, the names begin to be familiar.

So it may come as something of a shock to realise that no more evidence has been found for the lives and the achievements of David and Solomon, than for the tales of exodus and conquest that precede them.

This is not for want of trying. Both Christian and Jewish

archaeologists have sought assiduously in Jerusalem for evidence to corroborate the accounts in 1 Kings of Solomon's enormous wealth, mighty throne of ivory overlaid with gold, and superb temple – constructed by builders hired from Lebanon, and covered within and without in gold. So great was his magnificence that when the Queen of Sheba visited him in Jerusalem she remarked: 'I heard in mine own land of thy acts and thy wisdom. Howbeit I believed not the words, until I came, and mine eyes had seen it: and, behold, the half was not told me: thy wisdom and prosperity exceedeth the fame which I heard' (1 Kings 10:6–7). Alas, 'no trace has been found of that legendary king, whose wealth is described in the Bible as almost matching that of the mighty imperial rulers of Babylonia or Persia'.[4] There are impressive traces from earlier periods in the history of Jerusalem: but in the time of David and his son Solomon, 'Jerusalem … was more like a village'.[5]

As I shall seek to show in Part Three, the account by the Court Historian of the lives of Saul, David, and Solomon is a magnificent piece of writing. But history it is not.

Thus when we come to the big story – the core narrative – of the Old Testament, we find that its historical basis is pretty thin. What are the building blocks of this big story?

1. The story of Adam and Eve – no historical or archaeological evidence.

2. The story of the Flood – no historical or archaeological evidence.

3. The descent of the Israelites into Egypt, the Exodus from Egypt, and the wanderings in Sinai – no historical or archaeological evidence.

4. The conquest of the Holy Land – no historical or archaeological evidence

5. The events of the life of David (the fight with Goliath, the struggles with Saul, the seduction of Bathsheba) and of Solomon – the glories of the First Temple, the visit of the Queen of Sheba, the 700 wives, the massive international reputation – no historical, architectural, or archaeological evidence.

We should emphasise here that this 'demythologising' is as difficult for modern-day Israelis as for Christian believers in Biblical truth: the stories above provide for the state of Israel not only an intellectual justification, but a potent organising principle for the teaching of history, for the political life of the state, and for its military boundaries and policies.

6. The Old Testament as morality: what kind of god is God? What morality does the Old Testament teach? And is it 'right'?

A close look at the Old Testament shows that morally it is a very mixed bag. Stick in your thumb and you may get a plum – or you may lose a limb! Consider the ten statements below. Nine are from the Old Testament; one is not.

1. 'Therefore thus saith the Lord God ... because of all thine abominations ... the fathers shall eat the sons in the midst of thee, and the sons shall eat their fathers';

2. 'Because thou servedst not the Lord thy God with joyfulness, and with gladness of heart ... he shall put a yoke of iron upon thy neck, until he hath destroyed thee ... The tender and delicate woman among you ... her eye shall be evil toward the husband of her bosom, and toward her son, and toward her daughter, And toward her young one that cometh out from between her feet [the *New Oxford Annotated Bible* has 'afterbirth'], and toward the children which she shall bear: for she shall eat them for want of all things secretly in the siege';

3. 'Moreover of the children of the strangers that do sojourn among you, of them shall ye buy, and of their families that are with you, which they begat in your land: and they shall be your possession. And ye shall take them as an inheritance for your children after you, to inherit them for a possession; they shall be your bondmen [slaves] for ever';

4. 'If a man have a stubborn and rebellious son, which will not obey the voice of his father, or the voice of his mother ... Then shall his father and his mother lay hold on him, and bring him out to the elders of his city, and to the gate of his place ... And all the men of his city shall stone him with stones, that he die';

5. 'For that which befalleth the sons of men befalleth beasts ... as the one dieth, so dieth the other; yea, they have all one breath; so that a man hath no pre-eminence above a beast: for all is vanity';

6. 'Happy shall he be, that rewardeth thee as thou hast served us. Happy shall he be, that dasheth thy little ones against the stones';

7. 'A gift in secret [a bribe] pacifieth anger: and a reward [bribe] in the bosom, strong wrath';

8. 'And he took it, and the king thereof, and all the cities thereof; and they smote them with the edge of the sword, and utterly destroyed all the souls that were therein; he left none remaining ... but utterly destroyed all that breathed, as the Lord God of Israel commanded';

9. 'And the fear of you and the dread of you shall be upon every beast of the earth, and upon every fowl of the air, upon all that moveth upon earth, and upon all the fishes of the sea; into your hand are they delivered';

10. 'In the name of God, the lord of mercy, the giver of mercy. When God's help comes and He opens up your way, when you see people embracing God's faith in crowds, celebrate the praise of your Lord and ask His forgiveness: He is always ready to accept repentance'.

The odd one out, of course, is number 10, which is from the Qur'an.[6]

How can we make sense of these? If the Old Testament is a unity, which of these views represents that unified moral view? And if it is a multiplicity, which of its voices should we attend to?

Let us go back for a moment to Shakespeare, our other *Desert Island* companion. Shakespeare is a historical character who died in Stratford in April 1616; we have his will, we have the testimony of people who saw his plays and read his poems, and his works were published both during and shortly after his death. Yet the exact texts of Shakespeare's plays are a matter of constant dispute. There is disagreement about the wording as between the First Folio and the First Quarto. There are phrases that editors usually emend because the original doesn't make sense. There are passages that are notoriously difficult (does Gertrude really mean it when she describes her son as 'fat and scant of breath'? *Hamlet? Fat?*). There are lines that no one can make sense of (what does Hamlet mean when he says, 'The dram of eale/Doth all the noble substance of a doubt/To his own scandal'?). There are disagreements between critics as to which is the original version of some of the texts, there are disagreements about the order in which the plays were written, and there are plays (for example *Two Noble Kinsmen, Henry VII, King John*) where it is not clear how much if any Shakespeare actually wrote.

And all this says nothing about questions of interpretation: of how, once we have an 'agreed' text, we should actually make sense of it; of what it was, what it meant – or was supposed to mean – in its own time, and what it means now.

If this is true of Shakespeare, who died 400 years ago, how much more true will it be of the Bible, whose earliest elements date back 3,000 years?

The Bible is traditionally held – by Jews and Christians alike – to be the word of God, with every line divinely inspired and packed with meaning and guidance. On closer inspection, this is a difficult claim to maintain.

Some of the problems in the Old Testament are matters of sheer textual inaccuracy: cases where the text 'is carefully preserved even where it does not make sense'.[7] Misprints and omissions creep into typeset Bibles – see the two-page list of errors printed at the end of the first King James Bible, or the 1576 Version which contrived to omit a vital word in the seventh commandment, making Moses solemnly command his people to commit adultery. And if these occur in English versions, where they can be traced, we shall never know what errors, inaccuracies, transpositions, repetitions, omissions, and reworkings found their way into the texts in ancient times through the long process of copying by hand that brought them into recorded history.

Then there is the matter of moral inconsistencies: of passages where teaching seems frankly contradictory.

- Sacrifice: much of Leviticus and Deuteronomy – not to mention the later editorial work of Ezra – revolves around minutely detailed rules for sacrifice; yet we find the first Isaiah (writing in the time of Hezekiah, 715–687 BC, that is well before these writers), lamenting, 'To what purpose

is the multitude of your offerings to me, saith the Lord? ...
I delight not in the blood of bullocks, nor of lambs, nor
of goats ... Bring no more vain oblations; incense is an
abomination unto me' (Isaiah 1:11–13).

- Sexual morality: women in the Old Testament are seen
  as subordinate to men – fathers and brothers control
  daughters, sisters, and wives. This is a given in the Old
  Testament, whatever its compatibility with modern values, and is in fact more marked in the inheritance laws
  and practices of the Israelites than in those of the Near
  Eastern societies that surrounded them. Though some
  texts (Leviticus 20:10, Deuteronomy 22:22) assert that
  the death penalty for adultery is enforceable on men
  as well as women, it remains that women cannot enter
  the priesthood and their sexuality is more closely reg-
  ulated than that of men. But since the Old Testament
  – and especially the adultery commandment – is so often
  cited as a guide to morality, perhaps we may look at
  some examples of what is and is not allowed in specific
  instances.

a) The men of Sodom ask Lot to hand over his (male)
   guests so that they can have sex with them. Lot
   declines – but offers them instead his two (virgin)
   daughters (Genesis 19:8). Result: though the offer is
   not taken up, the Genesis writer seems in this particular case to approve of this behaviour.

b) Lot's daughters, thinking that they will not be able to find husbands, get their widowed father drunk and have intercourse with him, thus contravening Leviticus 18:6 and 9 but begetting children that will continue his line (Genesis 19:30–38). Result: approved again ...

c) The patriarch and prophet Abram (later to be renamed Abraham) enters Egypt as a pauper and encourages his attractive wife Sarah to enter Pharaoh's harem, describing her as his sister. Pharaoh gives him 'sheep, and oxen, and he asses, and menservants, and maidservants, and she asses, and camels' (Genesis 12:16). When the ruse is discovered, Abram takes Sarah back, despite her adultery, and returns with her to Israel a wealthy man (Genesis 13:2). Result: approved, at least for Abram (indeed he pulls off the trick again in Genesis 20).

d) Judah (founder of one of the twelve tribes of Israel and the person after whom the southern kingdom is named) has three sons. His eldest son marries a woman called Tamar. The young man dies, as does Judah's second son. Judah, as is customary, promises that he will give Tamar his third son in marriage – but delays. Tamar becomes impatient and decides to take the law into her own hands. Disguised as a roadside prostitute, she seduces her father-in-law Judah. Found to be pregnant and accused of harlotry, she shows in public the tokens Judah has given her, and success-fully forces him to find her a husband (Genesis 38). Result: approved for Tamar, despite Leviticus 20:12, which orders that intercourse between father-in-law and daughter-in-law is punishable by death.

e) Judah's second son Onan is asked to 'go in' to his dead brother's wife and 'raise up seed to your brother' – the so-called 'levirate marriage'. Reluctant to beget children who will not count as his, he 'spilled [his seed] on the ground' (Genesis 38:9). Result: he is struck dead by God, and on the basis of this text, taken to reveal a general law, Christian sects and faiths around the world (including of course Roman Catholicism) condemn masturbation ('the sin of Onan'), coitus interruptus, and birth control.

• Intermarriage with non-Jews: Moses' wife Zipporah is a Midianite, and both his father-in-law Jethro and his wife are faithful companions to him. Joseph (Genesis 41:45) and David (2 Samuel 3:2–5) also marry non-Israelites, and the Book of Ruth describes such marriage in deeply respectful terms. Obed, the child of the Moabite Ruth, becomes an ancestor of David (Ruth 4:17) and through him of Jesus (Luke 3:32). Yet intermarriage is forbidden in Joshua 23:12–13, Solomon is vigorously rebuked for 'mixed' marriages (1 Kings 11:1–8), and Ezra regards intermarriage as nothing less than a catastrophe (Ezra 9:1–4).

- Is it always important to tell the truth? Does it matter that Abraham (Genesis 13 and 20) and Jacob (Genesis 27 and 30) tell lies?

- Is God unique and alone, as the text constantly asserts – or is he one among many (Genesis 6:1–4, Psalms 82 and 86, Micah 4:5)?

- And finally, the biggest question of all. Given that (to take one example among many) God not only enjoins a complete massacre of non-Israelites (men, women, and children) when the Promised Land is invaded (Joshua 8 through 11), but slaughters no less than 24,000 of his own people for taking non-Israelite wives (Numbers 25:1–9); given that he promises that if Israel does not obey his law, he will 'rejoice over you to destroy you' (Deuteronomy 28:63); given that he threatens to make mothers kill and eat their own babies if they do not obey his laws (Deuteronomy 28:57) – in what sense can we speak of a loving God?

Now there are two ways in which we can look at inconsistencies and contradictions. One way is to assume that there is a single meaning and purpose behind all these texts, a recoverable 'right answer' to these puzzles: a single message, but a breakdown in transmission.

But what if there are different messages?

7. Who wrote the Old Testament? First attempts at a scientific reading[8]

Throughout the Middle Ages, the Christian Church (and Orthodox Jewry) held that the Old Testament was a unified work inspired directly by God. Scholars were aware from an early date of many of the inconsistencies mentioned above, but efforts to explore them were actively discouraged. To take but one example, the first five books of the Bible – referred to here as the Pentateuch – are also known as the Five Books of Moses. Moses is a major figure in these books, though the text never names him as the author. But in the 11th century AD a Jewish court physician, Isaac ibn Yashush, pointed out that the list of Edomite kings in Genesis 36 includes kings who lived long after Moses' death. The response to ibn Yashush was to name him 'Isaac the blunderer' and to suggest that his book should be burned. In the 14th century a scholar in Syria returned to these passages and suggested, apparently harmlessly, that perhaps they were written by 'a later prophet'. His work was reprinted with the offending passages deleted.

In the 16th century a Catholic and two Jesuit scholars (Van Maes, Pereira, and Bonfrère) repeated the suggestion that the Books of Moses consisted of the work of Moses with later additions, perhaps intended to bring place names up to date for later readers. Van Maes' book was placed upon the Catholic Index of Prohibited Books. And as late as the mid-17th century the Jewish philosopher Spinoza wrote, 'It is … clearer than the sun at noon that the Pentateuch was not written by

Moses, but by someone who lived long after Moses', supporting his argument with detailed evidence drawn from the books themselves: third-person accounts of Moses, the repeated use of the expression 'to this day', the references to Moses as 'the most humble man who ever lived' – and the fact that one book of the Pentateuch (Deuteronomy 34:5–8) describes Moses' own death! Spinoza had already been excommunicated from Judaism: now he was condemned by Catholics and Protestants, his book was placed on the Catholic Index, and an attempt was made on his life.

It is clear that there is something more than logic at work here …

However, the process of analysis and exploration did not stop, and during the 18th century, in the changing intellectual climate of the European Enlightenment, three independent investigators – a German church minister, a German scholar, and a French doctor – noticed, and connected, two features of the Pentateuch. One was the quantity of stories (about 25) that occur twice, known to critics as 'doublets'. There seem to be two versions of many Biblical stories, sometimes one after the other (two Creation stories), sometimes interwoven (two Flood stories), sometimes separated (two stories of Moses striking water from a stone at Meribah, two accounts of the acquisition of Shechem, two examples of Abraham lending out Sarah, two explanations about how Jacob passed on his inheritance to his children). This in itself is not particularly remarkable. But the 18th-century scholars also noticed that one version consistently referred to God as Yahweh – and the other would call him El or Elohim. Could it be that there were two sources for the five books of Moses – two writers? And if so, had someone rewritten the Bible by combining the two?

By the end of the 19th century the two sources had grown to five: J (the Yahweh writer – German scholars write it *Jahweh*), E (the Elohist), P (Priestly), D (for the Deuteronomist), and, for the final editor (or 'redactor') who pulled it all together, R. Sometimes these different writers (I shall assume that they are individuals: the evidence makes this plausible though not certain) wrote or collated extended parts of the present Old Testament; sometimes their work is intercut to form a single story from various parts, or juxtaposed so that one version leads directly into another. The best way to see this in practice is to take a familiar text: let us start with perhaps the most famous of all, the Creation story that opens the Bible. Here are the first five verses.

> 'In the beginning God created the heaven and the earth. And the earth was without form, and void; and darkness was upon the face of the deep. And the Spirit of God moved upon the face of the waters. And God said, Let there be light: and there was light. And God saw the light, that it was good: and God divided the light from the darkness. And God called the light Day, and the darkness he called Night. And the evening and the morning were the first day.' (Genesis 1:1–5)

Now let us move to Chapter 2 – the 'doublet' or second version of the story. It begins as follows.

'In the day that the LORD God made the earth and the heavens, And every plant of the field before it was in the earth, and every herb of the field before it grew: for the LORD God had not caused it to rain upon the earth, and there was not a man to till the ground. But there went up a mist from the earth, and watered the whole face of the ground. And the LORD God formed man of the dust of the ground, and breathed into his nostrils the breath of life; and man became a living soul.' (Genesis 2:4b–7)

These both tell the story of creation. But what a contrast in styles! The first is firm, measured, dignified, remote: the cadences are rhythmical; it lends itself to delivery from a pulpit. There are virtually no subordinate clauses; nothing is explained or justified, nor – since this God is self-sufficient and contains everything – does anything need to be.

Now consider the second. The creation of the world is relegated to a relative clause ('In the day that ...') that lasts almost two verses and is followed by a breathless explanatory sentence ('for the Lord God had not caused it to rain upon the earth') and a curious, rather unanchored contrastive ('But there went up ...'). There is a build-up in this passage, through these twists and turns, to something definite that is not revealed until the end of the extract. It is a general principle of grammar that main verbs govern sentences and are used for the most important event in the sentence. And what is it that the opening verses are building up to? *Not the creation of the world – but the creation of man.*

Let us look at both accounts in full. Here is the celebrated opening of Genesis.*

1. In the beginning God created the heaven and the earth.

2. And the earth was without form, and void; and darkness was upon the face of the deep. And the Spirit of God moved upon the face of the waters.

3. And God said, Let there be light: and there was light.

4. And God saw the light, that it was good: and God divided the light from the darkness.

5. And God called the light Day, and the darkness he called Night. And the evening and the morning were the first day.

6. And God said, Let there be a firmament in the midst of the waters, and let it divide the waters from the waters.

7. And God made the firmament, and divided the waters which were under the firmament from the waters which were above the firmament: and it was so.

8. And God called the firmament Heaven. And the evening and the morning were the second day.

9. And God said, Let the waters under the heaven be gathered together unto one place, and let the dry land appear: and it was so.

---

* I have left out the first part of Genesis 2:4 as this was inserted later by 'the redactor' (see page 40 above and Section 8 below).

10. And God called the dry land Earth; and the gathering together of the waters called he Seas: and God saw that it was good.

11. And God said, Let the earth bring forth grass, the herb yielding seed, and the fruit tree yielding fruit after his kind, whose seed is in itself, upon the earth: and it was so.

12. And the earth brought forth grass, and herb yielding seed after his kind, and the tree yielding fruit, whose seed was in itself, after his kind: and God saw that it was good.

13. And the evening and the morning were the third day.

14. And God said, Let there be lights in the firmament of the heaven to divide the day from the night; and let them be for signs, and for seasons, and for days, and years:

15. And let them be for light in the firmament of the heaven to give light upon the earth: and it was so.

16. And God made two great lights; the greater light to rule the day, and the lesser light to rule the night: he made the stars also.

17. And God set them in the firmament of the heaven to give light upon the earth,

18. And to rule over the day and over the night, and to divide the light from the darkness: and God saw that it was good.

19. And the evening and the morning were the fourth day.

20. And God said, Let the waters bring forth abundantly the moving creature that hath life, and fowl that may fly above the earth in the open firmament of heaven.

21. And God created great whales, and every living creature that moveth, which the waters brought forth abundantly, after their kind, and every winged fowl after his kind: and God saw that it was good.

22. And God blessed them, saying, Be fruitful, and multiply, and fill the waters in the seas, and let fowl multiply in the earth.

23. And the evening and the morning were the fifth day.

24. And God said, Let the earth bring forth the living creature after his kind, cattle, and creeping thing, and beast of the earth after his kind: and it was so.

25. And God made the beast of the earth after his kind, and cattle after their kind, and every thing that creepeth upon the earth after his kind: and God saw that it was good.

26. And God said, Let us make man in our image, after our likeness: and let them have dominion over the fish of the sea, and over the fowl of the air, and over the cattle, and over all the earth, and over every creeping thing that creepeth upon the earth.

27. So God created man in his own image, in the image of God created he him; male and female created he them.

28. And God blessed them, and God said unto them, Be fruitful, and multiply, and replenish the earth, and subdue it: and have dominion over the fish of the sea, and over the fowl of the air, and over every living thing that moveth upon the earth.

29. And God said, Behold, I have given you every herb bearing seed, which is upon the face of all the earth, and every tree, in the which is the fruit of a tree yielding seed; to you it shall be for meat.

30. And to every beast of the earth, and to every fowl of the air, and to every thing that creepeth upon the earth, wherein there is life, I have given every green herb for meat: and it was so.

31. And God saw every thing that he had made, and, behold, it was very good. And the evening and the morning were the sixth day.

Chapter Two

1. Thus the heavens and the earth were finished, and all the host of them.

2. And on the seventh day God ended his work which he had made; and he rested on the seventh day from all his work which he had made.

3. And God blessed the seventh day, and sanctified it: because that in it he had rested from all his work which God had created and made.

Now consider what immediately follows it (Genesis 2:4b–25).

4b. In the day that the LORD God made the earth and the heavens,

5. And every plant of the field before it was in the earth, and every herb of the field before it grew: for the LORD

God had not caused it to rain upon the earth, and there was not a man to till the ground.

6. But there went up a mist from the earth, and watered the whole face of the ground.

7. And the LORD God formed man of the dust of the ground, and breathed into his nostrils the breath of life; and man became a living soul.

8. And the LORD God planted a garden eastward in Eden; and there he put the man whom he had formed.

9. And out of the ground made the LORD God to grow every tree that is pleasant to the sight, and good for food; the tree of life also in the midst of the garden, and the tree of knowledge of good and evil.

10. And a river went out of Eden to water the garden; and from thence it was parted, and become into four heads.

11. The name of the first is Pison: that is it which compasseth the whole land of Havilah, where there is gold;

12. And the gold of that land is good: there is bdellium and the onyx stone.

13. And the name of the second river is Gihon: the same is it that compasseth the whole land of Ethiopia.

14. And the name of the third river is Hiddekel: that is it which goeth toward the east of Assyria. And the fourth river is Euphrates.

15. And the LORD God took the man, and put him into the garden of Eden to dress it and to keep it.

16. And the LORD God commanded the man, saying, Of every tree of the garden thou mayest freely eat:

17. But of the tree of the knowledge of good and evil, thou shalt not eat of it: for in the day that thou eatest thereof thou shalt surely die.

18. And the LORD God said, It is not good that the man should be alone; I will make him an help meet for him.

19. And out of the ground the LORD God formed every beast of the field, and every fowl of the air; and brought them unto Adam to see what he would call them: and whatsoever Adam called every living creature, that was the name thereof.

20. And Adam gave names to all cattle, and to the fowl of the air, and to every beast of the field; but for Adam there was not found an help meet for him.

21. And the LORD God caused a deep sleep to fall upon Adam, and he slept: and he took one of his ribs, and closed up the flesh instead thereof;

22. And the rib, which the LORD God had taken from man, made he a woman, and brought her unto the man.

23. And Adam said, This is now bone of my bones, and flesh of my flesh: she shall be called Woman, because she was taken out of Man.

24. Therefore shall a man leave his father and his mother, and shall cleave unto his wife: and they shall be one flesh.

25. And they were both naked, the man and his wife, and were not ashamed.

Each of these is a complete narrative of the creation of the world. But – as we have seen – how different! Let us first consider the direct contradictions.

a)   How long did God take to create the world? Seven days
     – or one?

b)   Did he rest at the end of the process – as in the first
     account – or not, as in the second?

c)   Which was created first? Plants – or man?

d)   Was man created in the image of God – or not?

e)   How was woman created? By the same process as the man
     – or by taking a rib from the man and creating woman
     from it?

f)   What relationship should man have with the animals –
     dominion, or a kind of observant curiosity?

Secondly, let us look at the differences – at what appears in
one story, but not in the other. The second account dwells on
the Garden of Eden – its location, its features, its details – and
on the plants and animals found in it: the serpent, the tree of
life, and the tree of the knowledge of good and evil. They are
what everyone remembers about the Creation story. *And they
do not appear in the first account at all.*

Thirdly, as we saw in our brief comparison of each
opening verse, the two accounts are written in a completely
different style. (Needless to say, the versions above are translations, but the difference in style is as apparent in the original
Hebrew as in English.) In the first we find a formal, orderly set
of co-ordinate clauses, the form used for statement rather than

for explanation (31 of the 35 verses begin with 'and'). This is the language of the sublime: the words of a writer, and a God, who knows what he is doing and feels no need to explain or justify himself. The second account is quite different stylistically. The language follows an elaborate, fluid structure, full of parentheses, contrastives ('But'), subordinating conjunctions ('For', 'Therefore') and afterthoughts. The writer takes pains to explain and justify his story.

Fourth, there are marked differences of attitude to the natural world. In the first, man is instructed to 'Be fruitful, and multiply' and to 'subdue [the earth] and have dominion over ... every living thing that moveth upon the earth'. Animals are not given individual identities; relationships are structured, controlled, and formal; God controls man (and woman, or 'female'), and the language used to address humans is identical with the language used to address animals: 'Be fruitful and multiply'. Male and female humans are created like male and female animals: as breeding pairs. In the second account, God begins by giving man 'a living soul' (2:7). He again creates animals – but the animals receive names (2:19–20). And who gives them their names? *Man.* And why is woman created? Not as part of a breeding pair, but because 'It is not good that the man should be alone; I will make him an help meet for him' (2:18).

And finally, if human relationships are different in the second account, so, dramatically, is the relationship between man and God. The first is the story of a remote, all-knowing God, awesome, majestic, and sacred in his power, but not someone to be engaged or reasoned with. And the second? Well, consider Genesis 2:19. 'And out of the ground the Lord God formed every beast of the field, and every fowl of the air; *and brought them unto Adam to see what he would call them*' (italics added). Man knows something that God doesn't; man can surprise God. God doesn't know what man is going to say – and is curious (one might almost say amused!) to find out. That would be completely unthinkable in Genesis Chapter 1. And how does God respond to the names man gives the animals? 'And whatsoever Adam called every living creature, that was the name thereof' (2:19). God cedes control to man.

I hope I have shown how very different these two accounts are – different in facts, different in emphasis, different in style, different in tone, and different in the kind of God they describe. What do we know about how and when they were written?

8. So – who did write the Old Testament?

As we have seen, the Old Testament begins with the five books of the Torah, and continues with the eight books of the Histories. These have justly been called the core Bible. Together they set out the mission of Israel, to be the chosen people of God; and they tell the story of how the Israelites won the Promised Land – and then lost it.

Amazingly, we know, with a high level of probability, who wrote these books – and much more important, we know why they wrote them.

There are five characters in our story, but before introducing them, I will set out the key areas of disagreement
between them.

The first arises from the political divisions between the
northern and southern kingdoms. Who is boss? And whose
culture heroes, and priestly families, will take precedence?
The Bible recounts that the northern kingdom (Israel) and the
southern (Judah) were united by David under one leadership
and at one capital (Jerusalem) around 1000 BC (2 Samuel 5).
David's son Solomon kept the two together, but with difficulty, and in the face of great resentment from the northern
kingdom, who felt – with some justice – that the kingdom of
Judah was taking much more than it gave. The relative status
of Israel and Judah, and of the mythical ancestors (the twelve
tribes of Israel) who validated that status, was much disputed.

The second is about sacrifice – and where it should be
carried out. Like many peoples around the world, the ancient
Israelites treated meat-eating as sacred: animals could not be
killed for food without performing a ceremony. There was no
disagreement about this, nor about the principle that a priest
should be involved to consecrate the animal and ensure that
the butchery was carried out to strict religious principles.
Disagreement centred on where that ceremony should be
carried out – and hence, on where farmers could kill and eat
their animals. Could it be at local centres – the so-called 'high
places' – where the local group of Levites (the priestly clan)
could officiate? Or must it be at a major religious centre, such
as Shiloh in the north, or Hebron or Jerusalem in the south?

This question of centralisation versus decentralisation came to be of enormous importance.

The third is about the status of Moses. Priesthood in ancient Israel was inherited and limited to the tribe of Levi. Although Moses (along with Abraham) was the great hero of the whole Hebrew people, there was a constant rivalry within the priesthood between the descendants of Moses (concentrated in the north) and the descendants of Aaron in the south, presiding over Judah from their sacred centre at Jerusalem. Both Moses and Aaron were too securely established as giant symbolic figures to be directly attacked: but a subversive power struggle between the descendants of Moses and the descendants of Aaron lies behind many otherwise inexplicable stories in Genesis and Exodus.

The fourth is spiritual: what is the nature of God, and how does man relate to God? Does God have human feelings and thoughts? Change his mind? Listen as well as speak? Learn from humans? Or does he speak from a great distance without the possibility that we can ever understand or fathom his greatness?

The fifth is about how the Israelites should relate to the peoples around them. Is intermarriage allowed, or not? There are absolutely radical differences between the Biblical writers on this point.

As we have seen, the core of the Old Testament lies in its story – God's mission for the Israelites, and their failure to carry it through. This has long been viewed as a single coherent unity: a unity of story, a unity of theme, and above all a unity of message. Behind this, of course, is the long-standing view of the divine origins and inspiration of the Bible.

The evidence does not support the view of a single unified text. Bible scholarship is an enormous field – dwarfing, for example, the shelves of books written on Shakespeare – so I shall be very selective, but I shall try to show that the first five books of the Bible represent, not one theology, but several: and not one unfolding story, but an entertaining and often intemperate set of arguments between different political and religious factions.

One of the most curious and exciting features of the OT is the fact that we know more about the people who wrote the Pentateuch than we know about the writers of the four Gospels. We can identify with some confidence the five authors who gathered, collated, and committed to paper – or rather to the rolls of papyrus that did duty in the ancient world for written documents – the stories that inform so much both of the religion and of the imagination of the modern world. These stories are now interwoven to form the continuous narrative of the Bible, which was for almost 2,000 years believed to be a unity not only in its form but in its composition. But they were originally entirely separate.*

Who were the people who wrote them?

---

* It is frustrating to discover that this knowledge has been around so long: it was possible to buy a Bible printed in different colours to show the different authors, the so-called Polychrome Bible, as long ago as 1893.

The first author, always known to scholars as 'J' because of his absolutely consistent use of YHWH (Yahweh, in German *JHWH*) for the name of God, is thought to have belonged to the royal court in the southern kingdom, Judah. Internal evidence within the text shows that he wrote after 842 BC (when Edom broke away from Judah after a six-year war of independence), and before 722 (when the northern kingdom of Israel fell to the Assyrians).

We owe to J the stories – or the adaptation of these stories from existing myths and legends of the Near East – of the Garden of Eden; Cain and Abel; the Tower of Babel; Potiphar's wife and her attempt to seduce Joseph; Moses and the bulrushes. The J author loved stories. But we also owe to J a particular concept of God: a god who is curious about humans (Genesis 2:19), who changes his mind (6:6), and who prefers mercy to justice (8:21–22).

We have said 'he', but the J author, uniquely among our authors, may have been a woman (the others were all members of the priesthood, which was restricted to men). Why do we say this? Not just because of his, or her, interest in character and narrative, but especially because of the story of Judah and Tamar (Genesis 38) in which a woman takes the initiative, breaks rules, and forces a man to admit that he is in the wrong.

Our second writer is from a similar period (9th or 8th century BC) – but from Israel, the northern kingdom. Scholars refer to him as E because his work consistently refers to God as 'El' or 'Elohim', in contrast to the usage of the J author. He seems to have been a Levite priest from Shiloh. We will have more to say about him later.

The third author, 'P' – the Priestly source – is closely associated with King Hezekiah, who ruled the southern kingdom of Judah from 715–687 BC, immediately after the fall of the northern kingdom in 722. Hezekiah introduced and carried through a policy of religious centralisation – notably of sacrifice – and of purification, and the P author greatly admired this.

We have already met the P author in our account of the Genesis Creation story above: firm, authoritative, unyielding. We meet him again after the Flood story: 'the fear of you and the dread of you shall be upon every beast of the earth' (Genesis 9:2). The watchword of the P author is implacable justice, administered through the hierarchy of the priesthood. There are no talking animals, no angels, no dreams: instead there is a huge body of instruction for the priests about how to carry out sacrifice, burn incense, and conduct oneself appropriately. The emphasis shifts from Moses the prophet (the northern hero), to the southern hero Aaron the high priest. In J, E, and D (see below) the words 'grace', 'mercy', and 'repentance' occur about 70 times. *In the whole of P they are not mentioned once.*

Our fourth author, the so-called 'D' or Deuteronomist, is also closely associated with a king – King Josiah, who ruled from 641 BC till 609 – and with a law code, Deuteronomy. The key theme of the Deuteronomist is the concept of the covenant, the bargain or contract between God and his chosen people. The special contribution of the Deuteronomist is to stress the cycle of infidelity–defeat–repentance–forgiveness that runs through the history of the kings of Israel and Judah, and their peoples, in their relationship with God.

The author of Deuteronomy was a priest from the northern city of Shiloh – and he is almost certainly the prophet Jeremiah, author of the book of the same name.

We will come on to the fifth author in a moment. But let us look at the relationship between the four writers mentioned so far.

J and E were parallel accounts: J from the south, E from the north. Not surprisingly, they had political as well as theological differences and points to make. The J author needed to justify the primacy of the tribe of Judah that ruled the southern kingdom of that name. Judah was traditionally the youngest of the four sons of Jacob with territory in the south. How could the J author justify Judah, a youngest son, taking precedence over his three elder brothers to become the ancestor of the ruling tribe? He made it clear in Genesis 49 that Judah's three elder brothers had all behaved inappropriately (in the case of Reuben, through sleeping with his father's concubine, a major error of judgement) and that Judah had received the birthright from his father. E makes no mention of this story.

What does E say about the same topic – the way Jacob bestows his birthright among his children? He makes no mention of Judah – why indeed should he? But he recounts in Genesis 48 how Jacob bestows special favour on his grandson

Ephraim. Why Ephraim? Because Ephraim was another name for E's home, the northern kingdom of Israel.

Needless to say, the Ephraim narrative does not appear in J.

The same pattern recurs with reference to the disputed city of Shechem, owned by the north but claimed by the south. Both writers mention the acquisition of Shechem from its Hivite inhabitants. The northern E writer says they paid its inhabitants a generous fee (Genesis 33:18–20). The southern J (Genesis 34) says they massacred them!

P, the Priestly author, working from an Aaronid perspective, wrote the largest part of the five books long attributed to Moses. What do we know about the relationship between the 7th-century P and the 8th/9th-century JE stories? We know that P was aware of J and E; that he based his story on the same episodes; and that he consistently retold those episodes so as to emphasise the role of Aaron and his descendants, to the extent of introducing the idea that Moses and Aaron were actual rather than metaphorical brothers, and omitting from his accounts all reference to sacrifice unless carried out by the Aaronid priesthood.

Why is he doing this? Why does P recreate as complete and separate units, not just the Creation and the Flood stories, but no fewer than 23 other parallel accounts of incidents in JE?

Because he wants to write a complete, self-sufficient text that will replace the JE Torah of Moses – with a Priestly Torah of Aaron.

What about our fourth writer, the Deuteronomist, whose work spans the period 622–587 BC? Did he know about the work of J, E, or P? He certainly did: he refers to incidents and ideas from each of these writers on a number of occasions. And did he have a view on them? Indeed he did. The Book of Deuteronomy is presented as Moses' farewell speech before his death. It restores Moses to pole position as the Hebrew culture hero – and makes virtually no mention at all of Aaron and the Aaronid priesthood, thus completely reversing the thrust of P a century earlier. He even refers to the P text in highly unflattering terms: 'the false pen of the scribes has made it [the Torah] into a lie' (Jeremiah 8:8, New Revised Standard Version).

So what can we deduce from the four compilers of the early part of the Bible? Of course all four agree on the sacred and political mission of the people of Israel, and on some kind of special relationship between God and his chosen people. But within this we find a high level of disagreement; a growing level of politicisation and sectarian infighting alongside their theological differences; and – in proportion as the kingdom becomes less powerful and independent – a tendency to move away from mercy and forgiveness, in the direction of justice and retribution.

So, what happens to this heap of conflicting and mutually contradictory scrolls? Will it be possible to rescue something from the wreckage? It is time to bring in our fifth writer, known to scholars as 'R' (for redactor, or editor).

Imagine you are standing in what looks like the book warehouse of a charity shop – perhaps Oxfam. Around you is all the jumble of books and magazines that find their way to second-hand shops; poetry and prose, history and fiction, Mills & Boon and Churchill's *History of the Second World War*, Shakespeare and Biggles, back numbers of *The Watchtower*, old royal biographies, railway timetables for lines that no longer exist. Some of the copies have pages or whole sections missing; none of the sets is complete.

Now stretch your mind a little more. Imagine that the charity shop exists in a parallel universe. Britain did not win the Second World War. Germany did. London was bombed flat, St Paul's and Westminster Abbey were destroyed, the royal family were executed and the Church of England despoiled and dismantled. A Quisling government runs the country under the watchful eye of Berlin. (Or, if you wish, Moscow.)

You thought your job was just to sort and price these volumes. But you're wrong. Your task is to use these materials, and only these materials, to write a history of England. The people who gave these books – precious books, in the present state of things – will want to see evidence that they are used: you can select and edit them, but you must make some reference to every one. And because there are no printing presses available to you for this task, you will have to write it – and have it copied – by hand, with all that that implies by way of errors, omissions, and duplications.

How will the finished work be judged? The scholar will ask, 'Is it complete?' The historian will ask, 'Is it true?' The preacher will ask, 'Is it good?' The literary critic will ask, 'Is it beautiful?' And the resistance fighter, dedicated to restoring the freedom and greatness of his (or her) country and fulfilling its mighty destiny, will ask, 'Does it support the struggle?' You must satisfy all of these.

That is the challenge that faces you. And that is what faced the person who pulled all the previous scrolls, all the earlier writings, into a single unity. Israel and Judah, the old kingdoms, no longer had any independent existence; Jerusalem had been sacked in 587 BC and its Temple destroyed; the leaders and opinion-formers had either been led away into captivity in Babylon or had fled to Egypt; the literary tradition was in pieces, the practice of the religion was fragmented, and those returning from Babylon in 538 BC found themselves scorned and rejected by their co-religionists still living in the ruins of the old city.

Somewhere around 460 BC, a Hebrew scribe at the court of Babylon brought to completion an extraordinary feat. He took the work of J, E, P, and D – texts that had been set up in many cases as mutually exclusive and antagonistic alternatives – and combined them into one continuous narrative. He took the P Creation story and the J Creation story and made them into Chapters 1 and 2 of Genesis, his opening book; he took the P Flood story and the J Flood story and wove them together so that the joins remained undetected for 2,000 years; he set a Priestly text at the start of each of the five books of the Torah; he inserted brief linking verses between the different materials to make the stories run smoothly on. And he did this, as far as we can tell, without taking out a single word.

Why did he do this? Why, if a unified version was needed, did he not just edit out the bits he didn't like? The answer is that he couldn't – the stories and the teachings were too well known. The Diaspora (scattering) of the Babylonian exile and the flight into Egypt had carried the earlier scrolls – the first 'biblia' – all round the pagan Near East, and as with the internet in our time, no censorship on earth could suppress them. So as he couldn't beat them, the Redactor – in every sense of the word – joined them.

There is relatively little of R's own writings in the Bible – most of his work consisted of discreet, sensitive, and highly flexible reordering. The structure he created, the apparent unity that resulted from it, and the skill with which he wrote, have created an extraordinary work that has held together for over 2,000 years. But the shape of the work, though unobtrusive, shows his intention and his values very clearly. He rearranged the material so that every one of the five books of Moses began with a Priestly text, showing beyond dispute that he came from the Aaronid priesthood.

Do we know who he was? Almost certainly we do.

Around 458 BC, a great Jewish scholar and scribe left Babylon, where a substantial Jewish community had been founded in the exile period and still lived on, to make the arduous four-month journey across the desert to the newly rebuilt city of Jerusalem. He brought with him a substantial returning group of exiles and carried rich gifts for the Jerusalem community from the Babylonian emperor Artaxerxes I. He described himself as 'a ready [skilled] scribe in the law of Moses' and as a direct descendant of Aaron (Ezra 7:5–6), and he came with 'the law of God' in his hand (Ezra 7:14). On his arrival, standing in the square before the Water Gate, he read a scroll to the assembled people of Jerusalem 'from the [early] morning until midday' (Nehemiah 8:3), and 'the people wept, when they heard the words of the law' (Nehemiah 8:9).

What was the book that moved them so powerfully? It was the Pentateuch, the 'five books of Moses', newly assembled from all the sources we have been considering above. Who was the reader? The reader was Ezra, author of the book of that name in the Bible. And we can make a very confident guess that he was also the Redactor – the man who, more than anyone else, was responsible for the shape and structure of the first five books of the Bible as we have them now.

The tradition that Ezra 'wrote' this part of the Bible goes back to the Fourth Book of Ezra, which dates from about 100 AD but is not included in the Protestant Bible. And Jerome in the 4th century AD writes of Ezra as 'the renewer of the Pentateuch'. Ezra himself hints, but does not say, that he is the Redactor. But he is very explicit about another of his actions. By his own account (Ezra 9 and 10) he persuaded the Jews of Jerusalem to dissolve all the marriages they had contracted with non-Jews, and to put aside not only the wives, but also the children, involved in these unions. He believed in racial purity; and he practised ethnic cleansing.

Before making our final comments on the OT we should look at two elements that we have not considered. The first is the 'begats'. Anyone who sets out to read the OT from end to end will find much of it numbingly repetitive and dull. The dullest parts of it, for the modern reader at least, are the interminable genealogies (the 'begats'), and the minutely detailed instructions, some for lay people and some for priests, about ritual and worship (the Holiness Code). Both are heavily represented in the Pentateuch. It is scarcely possible to make these interesting except perhaps to an orthodox Jew, but anyone wanting to understand the Bible must ask themselves why these mattered so much to the people of that time.

Traditional societies, whether in the ancient Near East or in our own time, place great store on genealogy and ancestry. In Britain access to the throne and to some seats in the House of Lords is by descent, and we have a strong tradition of respecting families whose connection with a particular piece of land goes back a long way: noble families indeed bear geographic titles – the Duke of Westminster, the Countess of Athlone – and newly ennobled commoners take a place name as a point of reference (Baroness Wheeler of Southwark, Lord Prescott of Kingston upon Hull). The world of the Old Testament Israelites up till 587 BC was a hereditary monarchy like ours with a similar emphasis on the 'birthright' of the first-born, but this emphasis on ancestry was strengthened by two factors that we do not share with it. First, as we have seen, the priesthood was also hereditary, so that priestly families could trace – or claim to trace – their paternity right back to Moses or Aaron. And second, perhaps even more importantly, was the connection between land and family through the system of tribes. That system had in practice ceased to operate by the time the OT was written down, but it continued to exercise a powerful influence nonetheless. The twelve children of Jacob formed, mythically at least, the original twelve tribes of Israel; most had ceased to have any geographical identity by the time of the Bible, but all had had land allocated to them by Jacob, and two (the southern Judah and the northern Ephraim) still kept that association and that entitlement.

That linkage is set out and defined in Genesis 48 and 49, but it becomes very real in Joshua 13–22 – supposedly recounting the events of around 1200–1300 BC, but probably dating from the 6th century BC – when the newly conquered Promised Land is specifically parcelled out, region by region, to eleven of the twelve tribes (the exception being the Levites, who as priests gain their portion through their share of the sacrifice).

The second element that modern readers find hard going are the ritual prohibitions that occur in substantial chunks in the Pentateuch – notably in Exodus 20–23 (the so-called Covenant Code), Leviticus (the Holiness Code, which takes up all 27 chapters), and Deuteronomy 5–26. The most famous of these are of course the Ten Commandments, which are repeated at least three times. However, they occur alongside a number of other prohibitions that seem less familiar to us. These include:

- Dietary prohibitions: the camel, the rock-badger, and the pig are unclean, as are the ostrich, the hoopoe, and the bat. Meat cannot be eaten together with dairy products. Locusts are acceptable, but 'all winged insects that walk upon all fours' are not. Fish that have fins and scales are fine, but not those such as eels that don't (Leviticus 11)

- Sexual prohibitions: sexual relations with close relatives are forbidden and adultery is punishable by death (Leviticus 18 and 20)

- Rules of farming: 'Thou shalt not plough with an ox and an ass [yoked] together' (Deuteronomy 22:10)

- Rules of dress: 'Thou shalt not wear a garment of divers sorts, as of woollen and linen together' (Deuteronomy 22:11)

- Rules of worship: 'He that is wounded in the stones [testicles], or hath his privy member [penis] cut off, shall not enter into the congregation of the Lord' (Deuteronomy 23:1)

What these strange rules have in common is a focus on *keeping separate*. They prevent things being mixed that should be kept apart. Camels, rock-badgers, and pigs are in some way anomalous (pigs, for example, have split hoofs but don't chew the cud); eels live in water but don't have scales like fish; a man's sisters and daughters are his relatives, not his sexual partners; mixing oxen and donkeys, or wool and linen, or meat and milk, or sexually ambiguous people with people of normal gender, brings together things that are different and should be kept apart.

The particular resonance of these laws for the Hebrews is that as things got worse for them politically – these laws date from the late 7th century BC, after the fall of the northern kingdom, and during the fundamentalist reign of Josiah – *they came increasingly to see themselves as a people set apart* (Deuteronomy 7:6). Their political troubles are seen as the result of falling down on their mission, and so there is heightened emphasis on not 'mixing themselves' with the peoples around them. 'I am the Lord your God, which have separated you from other people. Ye shall therefore put difference between clean beasts and unclean … And ye shall be holy unto me: *for I the Lord am holy, and have severed you from other people, that ye should be mine.*' (Leviticus 20:24–26, italics added) They are under orders, as God's chosen people and exemplars, to live exemplary lives: to keep themselves pure for God.

This is not about puritanism (which rejects pleasure); it is about perfectionism (which rejects impurity). Sacrifices are expected to be perfect animals without blemish (Leviticus 22:21) because they are offered to God, and the standards for priests are even higher than the standards for the laity, because priests are called upon to set an example to their own people. As the external threats increased, the Israelites became ever more focused on the separateness, and the need for perfection, of their religion, their nation, and their God; hence the appalled reaction of Ezra in 458 BC when he found that the Jews in Jerusalem were 'mixing themselves' with non-Jews.

Buried among these late 7th-century laws, with no special emphasis, are the rules about sex with animals (death to both parties) and sex between man and man (same punishment) – Leviticus 20:13–16. The context is identical: like eels, pigs, and 'insects that go on all fours', sex between humans and animals, or between man and man, is anomalous, and therefore unholy.*

9. Conclusion: if there is no single message in the Old Testament, what are its messages?

Grand – or grandiose?

Many aspects of the Old Testament make us think of it as 'ours'. The language, the imagery, the familiar stories and names – all these make it feel like a part of our culture, and indeed it has become such. But we should beware of seeing our reflection in it. We use its language for much of our morality, as if it was a social-democratic charter for the Western world. But it was written for a small, embattled people in a world without the United Nations or a police force, and the rules they lived by changed according to their circumstances. It was, as we have seen, the mission statement for the people of Israel – but the mission of the people of Israel is not a constant throughout the Old Testament.

In those parts of the Old Testament that were written earliest, the mission is broadly to establish God's chosen people – first to enable them to survive, and then to install them in

* Like everyone who writes about the Old Testament, I am hugely indebted to Mary Douglas and to Sir Edmund Leach for these insights into Jewish ritual prohibitions – a view that is now an anthropological commonplace but was revolutionary in its time.

their Promised Land. Their task is to obey God and their reward is to be loved by God (Hosea 14:5–7) and to settle, like contented hobbits, in their own country: 'they shall plant vineyards, and drink the wine thereof; they shall also make gardens, and eat the fruit of them. And I will plant them upon their land, and they shall no more again be pulled up out of their land which I have given them, saith the LORD thy God.' (Amos 9:14–15)

But this changes dramatically. By the time of the later writers, the mission is not to be civilised, but to civilise others: to be successful, not simply *among* the peoples of the region, but *over* those peoples, and to serve a God who rules, not just over them, but over all the peoples of the earth. 'For I will make you a name and a praise among all people of the earth' (Zephaniah 3:20, part of a post-exilic addition to the 7th-century original); 'His dominion shall be from sea even to sea, and from the river even to the ends of the earth … And the LORD shall be king over all the earth' (Zechariah 9:10 and 14:9: the early part of Zechariah dates from about 520 BC and these quotations are certainly later).

These references become much more pronounced in the latter part of Isaiah, the so-called Deutero-Isaiah (Chapters 42, 45, 48, 49, 54), composed in the Babylonian exile of 587–538 BC and subsequently edited, and in the last chapter we see not just world conversion – 'And I will also take of [the nations] for priests and for Levites, saith the Lord' (Isaiah 66:21) – but also world domination: a time when 'all flesh [shall] come to worship before … the LORD' (66:23).

What do we know of the history of Israel over this period? In the days of Hosea and Amos, the people of Judah were an independent nation, living in Judah (the southern kingdom) with an independent capital. By the time of the later quotations (all as far as can be ascertained are in chronological order), Judah had been overrun, the Temple had been destroyed, and the bulk of the population had fled or been exiled. All of these quotations date from that period, and are very specific to that context. *The more impotent becomes the reality – the more towering becomes the ambition.*

The religion of the underdog: four Old Testament themes

We should not leave the strange and various world of the Old Testament without drawing attention to the parts of it that hold constant throughout: four themes that emerge from the turmoil of conflicting attitudes. All four will have important implications when we move on to look at the New Testament.

The first is just to note how amazingly rustic and agricultural it is. Adam is told that 'in the sweat of thy face shalt thou eat bread' (Genesis 3:19). Leviticus doesn't just give you the Ten Commandments: it also tells you what to do when you find a straying ox or a fallen farm animal (in case you wondered, you should take care of them and seek to return them to their rightful owner). Tithes are paid in kind (grain, wine, oil) rather than money (Numbers 18:12). Rather than full of silver and gold, the Promised Land will be 'flowing with milk and honey'; if you besiege a town, you must not cut down food-producing trees that the besiegers or the inhabitants will need in future (Deuteronomy 20:19–20). (This prohibition is also made, and from a very similar agricultural context, in the Qur'an.) When the great prophet Balaam goes to visit King Balak, he shows his greatness by riding on a donkey rather than walking (Numbers 22); David, hidden in a cave, is close enough to Saul to kill him – but holds back – when Saul goes in to the cave 'to cover his feet', in other words to relieve himself (1 Samuel 24:3); the prophet Hosea describes himself as a cowboy, Amos as a shepherd and grower of figs. Despite the occasional digressions into the supposed wealth of Solomon, it is really all about peasant farmers.*

The second is the importance of social justice – justice to the weak, carried out, not in the hereafter, but in this world. Despite many and unpredictable digressions, both the priests and the prophets, whether pre- or post-exilic, keep coming back to this theme. It is primarily about 'widows and orphans' and the poor ('When thou gatherest the grapes of thy vineyard, thou shalt not glean it afterward [pick up the remnants]: it shall be for the stranger, for the fatherless, and for the widow. And thou shalt remember that thou wast a bond-man [slave] in the land of Egypt', Deuteronomy 24:21–22).

* As John Barton points out with reference to the Ten Commandments: 'This is the society of roughly the tenth to the seventh centuries BC ... [After the exile in Babylon] Jewish life in Palestine and in the communities of the Dispersion was no longer the life of a predominantly rural community ... They certainly did not consist of smallholders with a few cattle and some fields.' (Barton, *What is the Bible?*, 1997, pp. 94–5)

Two of Elijah's most significant miracles are carried out for a widow (1 Kings 17).

But it goes beyond this. Escaped slaves are to be protected ('Thou shalt not deliver unto his master the servant which is escaped from his master unto thee', Deuteronomy 23:15), and farmers are enjoined to be kind to the alien in their midst, even allowing them to rest on the Sabbath (Exodus 20:10). Even kings are forbidden to be excessively rich – 'But he shall not multiply horses to himself ... Neither shall he multiply wives to himself ... neither shall he greatly multiply to himself silver and gold' (Deuteronomy 17:6–20). And the prophets of Israel – Nathan, Ahab, Elijah, Ezekiel – use this ruling, this reminder that even the hearts of kings should not be 'lifted up above [their] brethren' (Deuteronomy 17:20), in defence of their own people and even, in the case of Uriah the Hittite, of the stranger.

This rough kindness even extends to slaves and farm animals: 'Six days shalt thou labour, and do all thy work: But the seventh day is the sabbath of the Lord thy God: in it thou shalt not do any work, thou, nor thy son, nor thy daughter, nor thy manservant, nor thy maidservant, nor thine ox, nor thine ass, nor any of thy cattle, nor thy stranger that is within thy gates'* (Deuteronomy 5:13–14). The 7th-century Jeremiah sums this up in Chapter 10 of Deuteronomy: 'For the Lord your God is God of gods, and Lord of lords, a great God, a

---

* It would be churlish to point out that the only person omitted from this rest period is the farmer's wife.

mighty, and a terrible, which regardeth not persons [treats all equally], nor taketh reward: He doth execute the judgement of the fatherless and widow, and loveth the stranger, in giving him food and raiment. Love ye therefore the stranger: for ye were strangers in the land of Egypt' (10:17–19).

Third is the conception of sin. It is important to understand that the Genesis narrative in the Old Testament does not function as proof of original sin. It is a story that is scarcely mentioned in the remainder of the Old Testament, and it is not about sin in the modern sense of failure to meet personal standards of conduct: of immorality, violence, untruthfulness, dishonour, lack of integrity. We have only to look at the lives of Abraham and Jacob to see that. Sin in the Old Testament is not primarily about morality. *It is, overwhelmingly, about obedience*. Virtue is following the commandment of God: sin is falling away from those instructions. The story of Kings and Chronicles follows a regular pattern: good kings did what God told them, bad kings didn't. And the most important thing that good kings did, was to centralise sacrifice at Jerusalem. Whether or not they were careful with their money or kind to their wives is irrelevant; David's unfaithfulness with Bathsheba was significant, but much less significant than his faithfulness to the will of God.

Nor is sin primarily personal. It is collective. Understanding this is the key to understanding why 'the sins of the fathers shall be visited on the children'. In a modern understanding of sin, it is incomprehensible that guilt should be passed down the generations: why, if I have led a blameless life, should I suffer the punishment inherited from my ancestors? The answer is simple. The commandments of God are about what a nation should do: about what the Israelites should do as the people chosen of God. And if they default, then they take on a collective guilt, and need a collective expiation.

Finally, this is almost entirely a religion of this world. The Promised Land is a real place, not a heaven: belief in the afterlife does not start to appear till the second part of Daniel, written after 200 BC. For the vast majority of the Old Testament the Israelites are commanded to live well in the world as it is; to believe that it can bring them happiness and fulfil their needs; to grow food, to bear children, to be merry, with 'wine that maketh glad the heart of man, and oil to make his face to shine, and bread which strengtheneth man's heart' (Psalms 104:15). The prophet Micah – a strikingly gentle voice among the furies of his fellows – puts it beautifully: 'For all people will walk every one in the name of his god, and we will walk in the name of the LORD our God for ever and ever … He hath shewed you, O man, what is good: and what doth the LORD require of thee, but to do justly, and to love mercy, and to walk humbly with thy God?' (Micah 4:5 and 6:8). For those who like to see a progression in religious thinking, we should remember that Micah (written in the 8th century BC) is some of the earliest writing in the Old Testament!

Does the Old Testament have a message?

'Seek and ye shall find – but only what you first put in.' It must be clear by now that beyond the four themes singled out in the previous section, together with its unswerving commitment to monotheism, it is meaningless to speak of a single message or a single morality in the 'instruction manual' of the Old Testament. If you look hard enough, you will find justification for any viewpoint or action. Certainly it contains the kind of humanistic, liberal messages that make it a suitable reference point for a so-called Judaeo-Christian morality. These humanistic messages are in it, but so are many others: you have to tune your radio to the wavelength you want to listen to. *The only authority in the Old Testament is the authority that we give it.*

PART TWO

THE NEW
TESTAMENT

'A Christian community that actually took as its
starting-point what can be known from the Bible,
read critically, rather than what has traditionally been
taught in the church ... is as far away as it ever was.'

(John Barton, *What is the Bible?*, 1997, p. 72)

1. The historical context: the world Jesus was born into (587 BC–1 AD)

We left the Old Testament in 587 BC, with the Israelites in a parlous state: their king dead, their capital destroyed, their kingdom overrun, and many of their people deported to Babylon: as Psalm 137 (and Bob Marley) has it, 'By the rivers of Babylon, there we sat down, yea, we wept ... How shall we sing the LORD'S song in a strange land?' The New Testament picks up the story almost 600 years later and recounts events from about 6 BC to about 100 AD. What was this world? What had changed over the intervening six centuries?

As we have seen, much of the consciousness of the Israelites, and quite probably many of their scriptures, were forged in the crucible of the Babylonian exile. However, that exile was not to last for ever. When Cyrus, King of the Medes and Persians, conquered Babylon 50 years later, he examined the case of the Israelites and very decently decided, not only to repatriate them to their own country, but also to allow them to take with them the confiscated gold and silver of their temple. Though the return was not an easy one (the books of Ezra and Nehemiah, though written a century later, show some of the difficulties), the city of Jerusalem was rebuilt, and a Second Temple was created on the site of the first. This Second Temple, improved and made more splendid over time, gave its name to the whole era between 536 BC and 70 AD.

Much could be said about these 600 years, but the task here is to explain the key events that determined the world, and the consciousness, that Jesus was born into. We can pick out five essentials that would have shaped his awareness: politics, economics, religion, geography, and what we may loosely call 'messianic expectations'.

The political context of Jesus' world was the continuing struggle to liberate the Jews from foreign rule. We have seen that the northern kingdom, the former Israel, had been lost as long ago as 722 BC – indeed it had become by Jesus' time the much-resented country of Samaria, whose people were condemned as heretics.*

For most of this period, the southern kingdom (formerly Judah, now known as Judea), and its capital Jerusalem, was controlled by outside powers. During this time Jewish culture was profoundly affected by the dominant culture of the Mediterranean at that time, the Greek or 'Hellenistic' set of values and practices. But despite this it remained proudly independent in its self-awareness and its political (and religious) ambitions. In 167 BC the Seleucid king (ruler of Alexander the Great's Eastern Empire) attempted to root out the Jewish religion and install statues of other gods in the Temple. The ensuing rebellion enabled the Jews to throw off foreign control and govern themselves under the Hasmonean dynasty from 140 BC through to 63 BC, when rivalry between different Jewish factions (a recurring theme) enabled Pompey to recapture Judea and bring in Roman rule. From this time on, Judea

---

* There is to this day a small population in Samaria who still follow their own interpretation of the beliefs, and the Bible, of that period.

was a Roman province, though it enjoyed complete religious freedom and was indeed largely ruled by a priestly aristocracy: the now-familiar term 'theocracy' was coined at this time by the Jewish historian Josephus to describe the government of Judea. Despite this, the memory of self-government was very strong, and the longing for it dominated both politics and religion.

The economic context is closely related to this theocratic method of government. The Romans always sought to govern through local power structures, and in Judea this meant ruling through the priesthood. The highly centralised structure of Jewish religion meant that wealth and power was concentrated in the Temple, and in the priestly families (headed at the time of Jesus' ministry by the High Priests Annas and Caiaphas) who ministered in the Temple and owned land all over Judea and Galilee. Herod, governor of Judea ('King of the Jews') from 37 BC to 4 BC, was not himself Jewish, but hoped to win the approval of the Jews through a magnificent rebuilding and expansion of the Second Temple. This was accomplished over an extended period, but required a huge amount of money to be raised by taxation, much of it collected from poor peasants working on land owned by members of priestly families. The resulting discontent led to a number of revolutionary movements that we will discuss below.

Third is religion (insofar as this can be separated from politics in a theocracy!). The practice of Judaism in Judea at the time Jesus was born was well established, at least in the urban centres, and securely based on the Torah – obeying the commandments and observing the purity and ritual laws of daily life. All these can be observed in modern Judaism. But within Judaism there were a number of religious groups active in this period, and we should single out four.

Three of them play important parts in the New Testament: Pharisees, scribes, and Sadducees. The Sadducees (tracing their origins to the High Priest Zadok and through him to Aaron, 1 Chronicles 6:4–8) were members of the priestly aristocracy, with largely conservative views. Alongside them we can identify 'scribes', likely to be of lower social status but still part of the religious establishment and equally traditional in their obedience to the letter of the Law. The Pharisees, by contrast, were a lay movement concerned to understand the Torah through discussion and debate (we may think of the Bible study groups of our own time). Many were quite senior in the priesthood (Joseph of Arimathea, for example, who gave his family tomb to house the body of Jesus), but Pharisees were closer to the synagogues, places of local worship, than to the Jerusalem Temple, and they were less tightly orthodox than their Sadducee and scribe co-religionists.

The fourth of these religious groups – not mentioned in the New Testament but certainly contemporary with it – were the Essenes, an intense monastic community set up in opposition to the Temple but seeing themselves as faithful to the principles and practice of the Torah. (The Dead Sea Scrolls discovered from 1947 on were the property of the Essene community of Qumran on the shores of the Dead Sea.) They represent one of the strands of the religious life of Jesus' time and it is quite likely that either he, John the Baptist, or both, would have been aware of their community, which was conservative in religious terms and in its interpretations of the rules of behaviour.

Fourth is geography. We have seen that the old united kingdom of Israel had long gone. In Jesus' time Samaria (the former northern kingdom of Israel) and Judea were governed by one of Herod's sons, and Galilee was under the rule of another. All these provinces had very different identities. Judea was the centre of the faith and the heartland of Jewish pride. Samaria had become the home of the hated Samaritans. And Galilee? Galilee had always had a reputation for being rural and remote. It also had a reputation for giving rise to rebellions – Judas the Galilean rebelled in 4 BC and he was not the first. And it was seen as rather comical: Peter is identified by his Galilean accent when he goes to find out where Jesus has been taken (Matthew 26:73), and Geza Vermes in *Jesus the Jew* (1973) recounts a number of scornful references to Galileans as backward and stupid. The tiny village of Nazareth where Jesus was born and raised was in the heart of Galilee, a fact that clearly did not help his credibility: 'Can there any good thing come out of Nazareth?', asks Nathanael in John 1:46. As we shall see, two of the Gospels go to great lengths to arrange for Jesus to be born elsewhere.

Finally there are what we have called 'messianic expectations'. Since the end of Hasmonean self-rule (140–63 BC), there had been a ferment of revolution in Judea and Galilee[9] and a widespread feeling that some kind of saviour – a 'messiah'

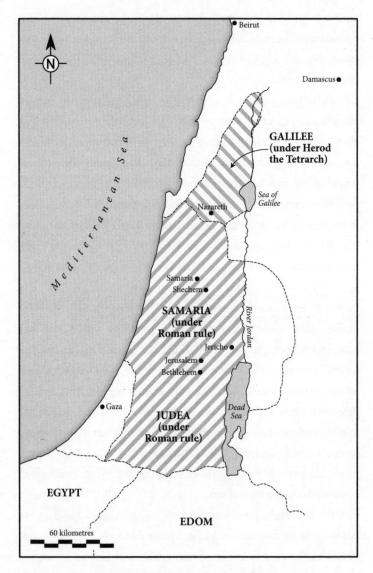

Diagram 6. Judea in the time of Jesus.

or 'anointed one' – was at hand to free the Jews from the yoke of Rome. Exactly what was meant by 'messiah' was not always clear. Was it a king who would take on the mantle of David? A liberator who would follow in the footsteps of Moses? A prophet in the mould of Elijah? No one knew, but there was no shortage of brave men – many from Galilee – to lead the movement of national liberation, nor of followers who rallied to their cause. The fact that the Romans hunted down and killed every one was not a deterrent.

That is the world – turbulent, rapidly changing, and intensely political – that Jesus would have been born into somewhere between 6 BC and 4 AD.

2. The structure and purpose of the New Testament: the mission statement for Christians

The New Testament consists of 27 books: four Gospels (Matthew, Mark, Luke, and John), the Acts of the Apostles, 21 Letters ('Epistles'), St Paul being the principal author, and finally the Revelation of St John the Divine. Though packed with meaning (much of it contested), the New Testament is only a third as long as the Old Testament.

The four Gospels tell the story of the birth, life, death, and resurrection of Jesus Christ – events that took place between about 6 BC and about 33 AD. The first three Gospels follow each other in content and in their picture of Christ, and are therefore known as the Synoptics (from the Greek 'synopsis' meaning summary); the fourth, John, tells a broadly similar story but takes a different view of the nature of Christ. Despite these differences, the four Gospels agree on certain fundamental facts: that Jesus was Jewish, that he was from a poor family, that he was brought up in a tiny village in Galilee, that he was baptised by John the Baptist, that he preached a generous and inclusive 'gospel' focused on the poor, that he performed miracles, that he had a struggle with the Jewish priesthood, that he was arrested with the connivance of the Jewish authorities, that he was crucified in Jerusalem by the Romans, that women followers found his tomb empty, and that he appeared to them and to others after his death in the form of a living person. Three of the four Gospels, as we shall see, also agree that he would appear again in the world within the lifetime of those who knew him.

The Gospels are followed by the Acts of the Apostles, written by the same person who wrote the Gospel of Luke (Acts 1:1–2). Acts tells the remarkable story of Jesus' followers from a key early meeting about six weeks after his death, through the spreading of the word to Jewish Diaspora congregations around the Mediterranean, the founding of a number of 'Christian' communities ('And the disciples were called Christians first in Antioch', Acts 11:26), and the development of the mission to Gentiles, right through to the arrival of Paul in Rome in the 60s AD, about 30 years after Jesus' crucifixion. Like the Gospels, it is told as a story: Peter and Paul survive stoning, lashing, imprisonment, shipwreck, and snakebite, there is much travel and many exciting escapes, and the character of Paul comes through very strongly.

Acts are followed by 21 Epistles. These are essentially guides to conduct, addressed to the early communities of believers in different cities and countries (the modern-day Syria, Turkey, Greece, and Rome). Each is a response to a different set of problems and challenges, often quite mundane – how to divide up believers' property, how to dress in church. They do not offer a fully worked out set of beliefs, but they do set out many of the basic values and proclamations that we take for granted now, and they contain some of the most celebrated passages of the whole Bible, familiar from weddings and funerals throughout the land ('For I am persuaded, that neither death, nor life, nor angels, nor principalities, nor powers, nor things present, nor things to come, nor height, nor depth, nor any other creature, shall be able to separate us from the love of God, which is in Christ Jesus our Lord', Romans 8:38–39).

A distinctive feature of the New Testament is its belief that the world would end soon and be replaced by a new heaven and a new earth (Revelation 21:1). In this it differs from much of the Old Testament, which is very 'this-worldly'. However, after about 250 BC a current of writing develops in the Old Testament, most notably in Daniel 7–12 (written during the Maccabean revolts of 167–160 BC), that announces the imminent end of the world. This 'apocalyptic' writing – or 'Jewish restoration theology'[10] – is very different from the gradual, 'here and now' process of bringing the world to God that is foreseen in the more familiar parts of the Old Testament. Even the wonderful

vision in Isaiah of the coming of divine rule on earth is of a
gentle kingdom introduced with love rather than with terror,
and consisting of a transformed yet still recognisable world:
'The wolf also shall dwell with the lamb ... They shall not
hurt nor destroy in all my holy mountain' (Isaiah 11:6–9). But
the vision in Daniel is more strange, more dreamlike, and
much more violent, than this: 'And four great beasts came
up from the sea ... The first was like a lion ... a second,
like to a bear ... another, like a leopard ... a fourth beast,
dreadful and terrible, and strong exceedingly; and it had great
iron teeth: it devoured and brake in pieces, and stamped the
residue with the feet of it' (Daniel 7:3–7). These beasts are
interpreted as earthly powers: 'The fourth beast shall be the
fourth kingdom upon earth, which shall be diverse from all
kingdoms, and shall devour the whole earth, and shall tread
it down, and break it in pieces' (Daniel 7:23). And the world
that they will usher in will not be one that we will recognise.

   This apocalyptic sense of an approaching end to the world
– prefaced with signs and wonders, and accompanied by huge
upheaval and suffering – runs through the four Gospels in a
way that makes them very different from the majority of the
Old Testament. All three Synoptic Gospels are shot through
with urgency because of the short time before the world ends
and all are judged: Jesus describes his own Second Coming,
and the end of the world as we know it, as due to happen
within the lifetime of those present (Matthew 24, Mark 13,
Luke 21). (It is not often realised that this features in the
Lord's Prayer. The phrase usually translated as 'Lead us not

THE STRUCTURE AND PURPOSE OF THE NEW TESTAMENT

into temptation' is now thought to be a request to be spared the approaching 'time of trial'.*)

John the Baptist, forerunner and perhaps mentor of Jesus, puts it crisply: 'Repent ye, for the kingdom of heaven is at hand' (Matthew 3:2). The same urgency runs through Acts (for example 2:17–21) and the Epistles: 'And the dead in Christ shall rise first: Then we which are alive and remain shall be caught up together with them in the clouds, to meet the Lord in the air' (1 Thessalonians 4:16–17).[11] And it provides the dominant theme of the Book of Revelation (Greek 'apokalypsos') that closes the New Testament, drawing heavily on the Book of Daniel to present its parade of beasts, horns, whores, virgins, horses, riders, swords, trees, trumpets, and lakes of fire, together with its complex and mysterious array of numbers – four horsemen, seven seals, 42 months, 1,260 days, 144,000 elect. The Book of Revelation concludes the New Testament with its promise that 'Surely I come quickly' (Revelation 22:20). Appropriately, given that the Bible opens with the Genesis story of Creation, Revelation book-ends the Bible with the creation of a new heaven and a new earth, 'for the first heaven and the first earth were passed away; and there was no more sea' (21:1).

In view of this belief, it is not surprising that the writers of the New Testament were on a mission to save the world.

---

* The word 'peirasmos', translated as 'temptation', has a meaning of 'testing' or (in a medical context) 'trial'. It is used in Revelations 3:10 to mean 'Last Judgement'.

But who was to do the saving? Who had the mission? We have seen that what Christians call the Old Testament is almost exactly the same book that the Jews call the Hebrew Bible; and we have seen in that Hebrew Bible God choosing the Jews as his special people and entrusting to them the task of bringing the world to him. Most of the New Testament is equally the work of Jews. Jesus was a Jew. The disciples were Jews. Though Mark and Luke may have been Gentiles, it is likely that Matthew and John, whoever they were, were Jewish; Jesus' brother James who headed the Christian community in Jerusalem after the death of Jesus was (of course) Jewish, as were the disciples; and we know that Paul, who wrote more Epistles than anyone else, was Jewish (and indeed a Pharisee) because he frequently and proudly mentions it. However, in the New Testament the work of bringing the world to God is deliberately linked to Christ – a figure whose divinity Jews do not recognise. The mission of salvation that was entrusted to the Jews is suddenly theirs no longer. It has been hijacked by the followers of Christ.

Not surprisingly, this presents a problem: as they used to say in the old Westerns, 'This town ain't big enough for both of us'.* If the task of saving the world has passed to the Christians, what is the task of the Jews? In different ways,

---

* As I write in August 2014, the same situation is repeating itself in the bitter rivalry between the new Islamic Caliphate, the Islamic State (or ISIS), and the older al-Qaeda, both dedicated to setting up an Islamic state under Sharia law.

this difficult question runs right through the New Testament, and as a consequence has structured, not to say poisoned, relations between Christians and Jews ever since. We shall look more closely at it below; for the moment let us simply note that in the course of the century or so after Christ's death, his followers explicitly claimed for themselves three roles that the Jews had formerly felt to be their own: chosen people, moral compass to the world, and spreaders of the word (evangelists, from the Greek 'bringer of good news').

3. The New Testament as history: is the story true?

> Christmas Eve, and twelve of the clock.
> 'Now they are all on their knees,'
> An elder said as we sat in a flock
> By the embers in hearthside ease.
>
> We pictured the meek mild creatures where
> They dwelt in their strawy pen,
> Nor did it occur to one of us there
> To doubt they were kneeling then.
>
> So fair a fancy few would weave
> In these years! Yet, I feel,
> If someone said on Christmas Eve,
> 'Come; see the oxen kneel,

'In the lonely barton by yonder coomb
Our childhood used to know,'
I should go with him in the gloom,
Hoping it might be so.

Thomas Hardy's poem expresses a very familiar hope. The
New Testament story is so beautiful: can't it also be true?

Despite the broad consensus in the Gospels about the
outlines of the life of Jesus, the four evangelists disagree with
each other on many points of fact (the philosophical and theological disagreements we shall come to later). Where in Judea
did Jesus' family come from? Who were his ancestors? Where
was he born? Which miracles did he perform? What were the
names of the twelve apostles? How many times did Jesus go up
to Jerusalem? What happened at his trial? What happened at
his resurrection? When and where did the risen Christ appear?
There is major disagreement on all these points.

The first point is to ask what we mean by 'true'. 'Truth'
in the sense of 'historical truth', correspondence to the facts,
is a key value for contemporary readers. But when we try to
view the New Testament from the standpoint of the modern
historian, we must realise that 'history' and 'truth' had very
different meanings to the Gospel writers than they do to us. As
Reza Aslan points out, 'Luke would have had no idea what we
in the modern world even mean when we say the word "history". The notion of history as a critical analysis of observable
and verifiable events in the past is a product of the modern
age; it would have been an altogether foreign concept to the

gospel writers for whom history was not a matter of uncovering *facts*, but of revealing *truths*.'[12] As Paul Beeching puts it in *Awkward Reverence*, 'Gospels are not historical accounts … in the modern sense of history as a documented account of the past. Gospels are primarily preaching devices intended to preserve and strengthen the reader's faith … they are not reports of historical events or accurate transcripts of ancient speech. To ask about the truth of Mark is akin to asking about the truth of *Hamlet*'.[13]

And if this is true of the Gospel writers, it is equally true of the early readers of the Gospels – those for whom they were written, and who shared the assumptions and conventions of the writers. 'The readers of Luke's gospel, like most people in the ancient world, did not make a sharp distinction between myth and reality … they were less interested in what actually happened than in what it meant.'[14]

Here is a small illustration: apparently trivial, but actually very revealing. All four Gospels assert that at the end of his life, Jesus and his disciples make a triumphant entry into Jerusalem at the time of Passover – a time when the city was crowded, heaving with pilgrims in a high state of religious excitement. All four accounts specify that he rides in 'on a donkey'. Since all four agree, we might put this down as a historical fact: an outward-facing 'truth of correspondence' – because it corresponds with reality – rather than an inward-facing 'truth of meaning', something that highlights the symbolic significance of the event. But one of the accounts goes a little further. Matthew writes that Jesus enters Jerusalem on two animals:

'And they brought the ass, and the colt, and put on them their clothes, and they set him thereon' (Matthew 21:7). This spectacular manoeuvre has survived all the editing and rewriting that every one of the Gospels has undergone: no scribe has seen fit to amend it. And this is for a very good reason. Whether or not Jesus actually entered Jerusalem astride a donkey (or astride two donkeys), the donkey is of vital importance because it connects Jesus to an Old Testament prophecy – one that only Matthew mentions, but all four evangelists certainly knew: 'Behold, thy King cometh unto thee ... lowly, and *riding upon an ass, and upon a colt the foal of an ass*' (Zechariah 9:9, italics added). The narrative connects Jesus with Zechariah's prophecy (5th century BC) of a triumphant yet peaceful king of Israel who 'shall speak peace to the heathen' and whose dominion 'shall be from sea even to sea, and from the river even to the ends of the earth' (Zechariah 9:10).

Casting Jesus as the fulfilment of that prophecy is a way of saying to the assembled pilgrims that their new king – peaceful, but all-powerful – has arrived. Matthew's knowledge of the rhetoric of the Hebrew Bible was limited and he (unlike the other three evangelists) did not realise that Zechariah was using techniques of parallelism that go back through the Bible to Canaanite literature a thousand years before, whereby a phrase is repeated in a slightly different form for emphasis; in this case only one donkey is involved. But what makes this detail revealing is that *it doesn't matter whether Jesus actually rode a donkey (or two donkeys) on his way into Jerusalem*. It didn't matter to the Gospel writers, and it didn't matter to their readers.

What mattered to writer and reader alike is not the fact, but the symbol. The facts are subservient to the fulfilment of the prophecy.

With the donkey and its foal in mind, let us look at five areas where the Gospels contradict each other, and/or the facts of history as we know them: the birth of Jesus; the use of Old Testament texts as prophecies of the coming messiah; the part played by the Jews, and the Pharisees, in the Gospels; the trial of Jesus; and the predictions of the imminent end of the world. We shall end by setting Acts alongside the Epistles, and asking: was St Paul a reliable witness to the facts of his own life?

A virgin birth?

Two of the Gospels (Mark, the earliest, and John, the latest) have no mention of the early years: Jesus first appears as an adult about to be baptised by John the Baptist, and his mother is mentioned in a perfectly normal context along with his numerous brothers and sisters. But Matthew and Luke provide very detailed accounts of his miraculous birth and indeed of his ancestry, and these accounts do not fit well with each other.

Matthew's Gospel begins with a detailed genealogy for Jesus tracing him through his father Joseph right back to Abraham by way of King David. He then recounts a virgin birth preceded by an annunciation from the Angel Gabriel. The birth in Bethlehem is followed by a visit from the Wise Men, a warning from God to take flight into Egypt, Herod's Slaughter of the Innocents, and in due course a return from

Egypt to a new village, Nazareth in Galilee. The story (as so often in Matthew) is constantly buttressed by references to the fulfilment of Old Testament prophecies.

Luke begins with not one, but two miraculous conceptions. The first is that of John the Baptist, whose parents are barren and 'well stricken in years';* the second is that of Jesus himself. Both are announced by angels; in an added twist, the mothers are cousins (Luke 1:36) and meet before the babies are born, with the Baptist's mother Elizabeth acknowledging Mary as 'the mother of my Lord' (1:43). The birth of Jesus takes place in Bethlehem. So far, so good. However, Luke goes on to give a different genealogy from Matthew (Luke 3:23–38) and a totally different explanation of why the family are in Bethlehem. According to Luke, the family originate in Nazareth (the village where they end up in Matthew's account), but go to Bethlehem because they are required to do so for census purposes as it is 'a city of David' and Joseph is 'of the house and lineage of David'. When they get there, there is 'no room at the inn' and Mary has to lay the baby Jesus 'in a manger', where he is visited by shepherds. There is no mention of stars, of Wise Men, or of Herod and the massacre of the little children, nor of the consequent need to take refuge in Egypt.

* This is a common form of miraculous birth in the Bible: Abraham's son Isaac, and the early hero Samuel, are born in similar circumstances.

There is no possibility that these stories are 'true' in the sense of representing historical events. This is not because of the angels and the star – the miraculous bits. It is because the non-miraculous elements – the genealogies, the dates, the explanations, even the geography – are donkeys and foals, conveniently placed to meet a literary and symbolic need. The evidence for this is overwhelming and I will limit myself to a few examples.

First, genealogy. The people of Israel had a clear expect-ation that the new messiah must be born in the town of Bethlehem (Micah 5:2) and be descended from David. As we have seen, they also had a pretty low opinion of Galilee (see John 1:46, 'Can there any good thing come out of Nazareth?').

Jesus is challenged on this point in John's Gospel (John 7:41–52), and can't give an adequate response; Mark makes no mention of it at all. Matthew and Luke, in differ-ent ways, set out to put things right. Matthew (1:1–17) gives Jesus a complete genealogy including David and Abraham – arranged in three groups of fourteen (David's name has a special relationship with the number fourteen), and including women and Gentiles (which reflects the importance of both groups in the early Church). Luke, however, has a different genealogy: it includes David and Abraham, but otherwise fol-lows a different route beyond Abraham right back to Adam, the first man and 'Son of God' (Luke 3:38). The point is that the genealogies are not matters of fact, but of meaning: they are there to show why Jesus fulfils a destiny, not to authenticate his birth certificate.

What of Bethlehem? Both Matthew and Luke have birth narratives, and both place the birth in Bethlehem: Matthew says that Mary and Joseph lived there, Luke says that they went there from Nazareth because of a Roman census that required everyone to go back to his town of origin. Both stories can't be true, and in fact neither is. Luke's references to Caesar Augustus and Quirinius, though plausible, are in fact historically wrong;[15] moreover no Roman census required anything like this, as it would have paralysed the economy of any country where it was applied.

Matthew uses different devices to connect Jesus to the great traditions of the Hebrew Bible. He makes Herod kill the firstborn of Bethlehem, and sends the holy family to Egypt to escape death. (It is curious that in the long catalogue of cruelties associated with Herod there is no other mention of this incident.) The associations of miraculous birth, killing of the firstborn, and escape into and out of Egypt, elegantly link Jesus with Moses, who – like Jesus – brought his people out of captivity in ... Egypt. The symbolism is magnificent: but the idea that a poor peasant family could make the long journey to and from Egypt, and then relocate to a wholly different part of Palestine, does not stand up to scrutiny.

There are three further points that emphasise the mythical, rather than historical, point of the virgin birth. The first is that only Matthew and Luke refer to it. No other New Testament writer does so – and that includes the Epistle of James, who as Jesus' brother might be expected to speak with some authority on the subject. The second is that it is not integrated into the narrative of Matthew and Luke after those opening chapters: for example, despite the fact that Mary, mother of Jesus, is described as the cousin of John's mother Elizabeth (Luke 1:36), when the two men meet as adults there is no indication in any of the Gospels that either knows the other. (The symbolic importance of the pre-birth meeting in Luke is to assert the superiority of Jesus over John – a much contested point at the time the Gospels were written.) In accounts dedicated to proving against all the counter-evidence that the crucified Jesus is the messiah promised by God, it seems rather odd that the most powerful, and indeed the unique card – his miraculous birth – is never subsequently played.

The third point is quite a shocking one. It hangs on two Hebrew words – 'aalmah' meaning 'young woman', and 'bet-ulah' meaning 'virgin'. The virgin birth described in the New Testament, result of a conception without sexual activity, takes its inspiration from the famous lines in Isaiah 7:14, 'Behold, a virgin shall conceive, and bear a son, and shall call his name Immanuel'. As it happens this is not a messianic prophecy but a political one: the prophet, writing in the 7th century BC, is assuring King Ahaz that his enemies will soon be cast down ('the land that thou abhorrest shall be forsaken of both her kings', Isaiah 7:16). But the accounts in Matthew and Luke take it to be messianic and treat the birth as a fulfilment of that prophecy, and a virgin birth has entered the dogma of virtually all Christian churches (with the honourable exception of the Unitarians).

Bible scholars have known for well over a century that the word 'virgin' is a mis-translation. The version of the Bible that the Greek-speaking Matthew and Luke referred to was the Septuagint, a Greek translation of the Hebrew Bible carried out around 180–150 BC. In the Septuagint, the Hebrew word is translated as 'parthenos', or virgin. But that translation is mistaken. The Hebrew word in Isaiah 7:14 is 'aalmah' (young woman), not 'betulah' (virgin). Isaiah makes no mention of a virgin, or of a miraculous birth: he simply says that a young woman will have a baby. The Septuagint is in error. This is perhaps surprising, rather than shocking. What is shocking is that after a brief flurry of 'young women', a number of American Bible editions – for example the 2001 'English Standard Version', reprinted in England in 2002 – have deliberately reverted to using the word 'virgin'.[16]

We should note at this point that what I have written here, though uncomfortable for those who take a literal view of Bible truth,* would not be taken as a criticism by Matthew and Luke. They would have been perfectly well aware that the plausible narratives that they had put together were not 'historical' in the modern sense. They would not have thought of this as 'real' history, as correspondence to fact. For them it was correspondence to truth – a story that revealed the reality behind the facts, the meaning behind the façade. As Paul Beeching puts it, 'Contrary to the impression many preachers

---

* Including Pope Benedict: see Joseph Ratzinger, *Jesus of Nazareth: The Infancy Narratives*, 2012, pp. 51–7, and my review on amazon .co.uk.

leave with their hearers, [the] New Testament was a product of the church, rather than the reverse'.[17]

Does the Old Testament predict a crucified messiah?

It is a principle of the New Testament that it seeks to build on the Old and to represent the Old Testament as predicting, or 'prefiguring', events in the New. The primary way in which it does this is through the device of 'fulfilment': we constantly encounter formulae such as, 'That it might be accomplished as it was foretold in the Scriptures ... As it is written in the prophet Isaiah ... All this took place to fulfil what had been spoken by the Lord through the prophet ... The Son of Man goeth as it is written of him'. This use of 'prooftexts' (Old Testament verses or stories that are used as prophecies or 'proof' of events in the New) runs through the Gospels; the virgin birth (as we have seen), the miracles, the rising again on the third day, and overwhelmingly the idea of a messiah – all these are constantly explained as fulfilments of something predicted by the Old Testament prophets. And they are equally important in Acts and the Epistles; lengthy discourses (for example, Acts 2:25–36, 7:51–53, 8:32–35) are devoted to showing how the Hebrew Bible foretells the events of Jesus' life, and in particular the idea of a suffering, crucified, and resurrected messiah.

There are many kinds of messiah in the Hebrew Bible, but unfortunately the crucified and resurrected messiah is not one of them. The scholarship of the evangelists was very incomplete, and their knowledge of the Hebrew Bible, though passionate, very faulty: Reza Aslan refers to Simon Peter (and subsequently

Stephen) 'displaying the reckless confidence of one unschooled and uninitiated in the scriptures' when they speak of the way Jesus fulfils Old Testament predictions.[18] Paul Beeching rather delightfully goes even further: 'Along with the Jewish teachers of their day, the evangelists feel free to wrench any passage they wish from the Hebrew or the Septuagint Greek scripture and to use it as a prophecy fulfilled in their narrative. In fact they will go further and misquote scripture or distort it to make their point. *If college students were to do what the evangelists do, we would fail them.*'[19] Beeching's point is particularly evident when it comes to the status of Jesus as messiah. This is broadcast all over the New Testament, and supported by claims that the suffering and risen messiah is foretold in the Scriptures. *But he isn't.* As Aslan points out:[20] 'In the entirety of the Hebrew Bible there is not a single passage of scripture or prophecy about the promised messiah that even hints at his ignominious death, let alone his bodily resurrection.'*

---

* Christians make much of a number of Old Testament texts – particularly the Suffering Servant passages in Isaiah 53 – which likewise date from the 6th or 7th century BC and supposedly predict a gentle and suffering messiah. However, Isaiah 53:7 ('he is brought as a lamb to the slaughter, and as a sheep before her shearers is dumb, so he openeth not his mouth') has also been held to represent Moses, Israel, the process of exile, the prophet Jeremiah, King Josiah, and King Jehoiachin. If the passage can bear such a broad interpretation it is hardly likely to have the narrow focus and predictive detail needed to make it prefigure the events of Jesus' life. It would certainly not have been seen in this way by a 1st-century Jewish readership.

What is particularly important is not what we think in the 20th century, but what the contemporaries of Paul (and Jesus) would have thought. And we can be very confident, despite the best efforts of the evangelists and the writers of the Epistles, that their contemporaries did not expect either a crucified, or a reborn, messiah. The only thing that might have impressed their Jewish audience was the miraculous birth – and that is the one thing that Peter, Stephen, Paul, and all the preachers in the first generation after Jesus (that is, before the Gospels were written) never mention.

Jewish opposition to Jesus?

A dominant theme in all four evangelists, and in the Acts of the Apostles, is the assertion that certain elements of Jewish society and politics resisted, undermined, and in the end actually killed Jesus.

The treatment of the Jews in the New Testament is unremittingly hostile. The evangelists constantly complain that the Jewish establishment gangs up on Jesus both in Galilee and in the Temple in Jerusalem, where there are a number of attempts to challenge and humiliate Jesus and even to betray him to the Romans (see for example the famous question about Caesar's image on the coin). Luke (20:20) speaks of 'spies' sent by teachers of the Law and the chief priests; the accounts in Matthew 22:15–22 and Mark 12:13–17 describe the questioners as 'Pharisees and Herodians'. And John goes even further, writing on occasion as if the Jews were an alien community: at one point (John 6:4) he explains that the Passover is 'a feast of the Jews'! As we shall see, this hostility reaches a point where 'the chief priests and the scribes sought how they might take him by craft, and put him to death' (Mark 14:1).

This hostility is rather peculiar for a variety of reasons. First, Jesus and all the apostles are themselves Jews. Second, Jesus unhesitatingly quotes and approves the Hebrew Bible – 'Think not that I am come to destroy the law, or the prophets: I am not come to destroy, but to fulfil. For verily I say unto you, Till heaven and earth pass, one jot or one tittle shall in no wise pass from the law, till all be fulfilled' (Matthew 5:17–18). (Calling this address 'the Sermon on the Mount' connects it with the Old Testament account of Moses receiving the Ten Commandments on Mount Sinai.) Third, the evangelists lump together supposed enemies of Jesus – for example, scribes and Pharisees – who would be very unlikely to get on or have a common cause (see above). Indeed, as E.P. Sanders puts it, 'Pharisees did not organise themselves into groups to spend their Sabbaths in Galilean cornfields in the hope of catching someone transgressing (Mark 2:23ff), nor is it credible that scribes and Pharisees made a special trip to Galilee from Jerusalem to inspect the hands of Jesus' disciples (Mark 7:2)'.[21] Fourth, the Pharisees in Luke's Gospel actually help Jesus by trying to persuade him to escape when threatened (Luke 13:31). And finally, the post-Jesus Church continued to use Jerusalem as its headquarters, and the Temple as its place of worship, throughout the period from Jesus' death in the early 30s right through to the destruction of the Temple in 70 AD.

Accounts of Jewish opposition to Jesus come to a frightening climax in the events leading up to and including the trial, and it is to this that we now turn.

What do we know about the trial of Jesus?
All four Gospel narratives have a broad framework in common. The main events, spread over a packed 24 hours, are:

- Jesus eats a 'Last Supper' with his disciples

- He is arrested at night in the garden of Gethsemane, but his companions are not

- He is questioned by the high priest

- He is taken to Pontius Pilate and questioned again

- He is scourged (a brutal lashing of 39 strokes with a leaded cat o' nine tails)

- Pilate offers to a Jewish crowd the choice to release either the prophet Jesus or the robber Barabbas, and the crowd choose Barabbas

- Pilate sends Jesus to be crucified

Christian religions see this as a coherent story that could plausibly report real events. But closer analysis casts much of this into question. Four writers – Geza Vermes, Robin Lane Fox, E.J. Bickerman, and Paula Fredriksen – have given this particular attention.

Geza Vermes (author of the seminal *Jesus the Jew*, 1973) draws attention to the difference between the timing given by the Synoptics (Matthew, Mark, and Luke), and that reported by John. The Synoptics place the Last Supper on the Friday night preceding the Passover, which gives it a powerful and beautiful symbolic force. On that Passover evening Jews slaughter a lamb in memory of the slaughter of Pharaoh's firstborn (Exodus 12:1–14) and God's rescue of his people from Egypt, making Jesus a symbolic lamb, slain to purchase the rescue of his people from a symbolic Egypt of sin and exile from God.

The first difficulty is with the Last Supper itself. The phrases, 'Take, eat, this is my body … This is my blood … Drink ye all of it' (Matthew 26:26 and 27) would be unexpected – not to say rather queasy – for a Jewish audience. The idea of the ritual slaughtering and eating of the god is very familiar in the pagan world, notably in Mithraism, but completely unknown in the Hebrew world of the time, and indeed very antithetical to everything the Bible commands: the whole process of kosher killing that controls Jewish dietary laws to this day (Leviticus 17:10–16) is designed to ensure that Jews never have to consume blood.*

The second difficulty is with the timing, and with what follows on from that timing. The three Synoptics – placing the Last Supper on the eve of Passover – then have Jesus arrested

---

* This lies behind the refusal of contemporary Jehovah's Witnesses to accept blood transfusions, as they take it that both the Old and the New Testament forbid the ingestion of blood in any form.

in the garden of Gethsemane and brought in front of the Sanhedrin, the court of 71 Jewish elders, in the small hours of the following morning, the early hours of Passover itself. The Sanhedrin question Jesus thoroughly and sentence him to death, but as the Romans did not allow the Jewish authorities to carry out the death penalty, these authorities send Jesus on to Herod with a request that he will question him, find him guilty, and execute him.

There are three problems about this. One is that the Jewish court procedure recorded by the Synoptics was nothing like the standard procedure laid down for such trials in Jewish documents of the time, which involved a thorough process of checking witness statements and verifying accusations, and which mandated a 24-hour 'cooling-off period' between judgement and execution.

The second is that it would have been completely impossible for the Sanhedrin to meet on that Passover eve and morning. It was utterly forbidden for such a court to meet on any Sabbath, but least of all on the Passover Sabbath.[22] And even if an exception had been made, it would have been impossible to get the elders together in one place because of their heavy commitments to their Passover duties in the Temple – duties that had exercised them for a number of days beforehand and would continue to occupy them throughout that day. (Imagine assembling the full Council of Cardinals, or the entire Synod of Bishops, on Easter morning and without any prior notice.) As Vermes judiciously puts it, 'the timing of the events in the Synoptic Gospels is quasi impossible'.[23]

And the third problem is simply this: the offence that Jesus was accused of, and that seemingly caused the high priest to rend his clothes and cry blasphemy, was not an offence, and not a blasphemy. As Paula Fredriksen remarks: 'We have ample record in Josephus of other self-proclaimed messianic figures in the period leading up to and including the revolt; later, we have the example of Bar Kokhba ... nowhere are the claims seen as blasphemous'.[24] Moreover, if it had been blasphemous, there was a recognised punishment for that particular crime, namely stoning – which, as we see from Acts 7:57–60, the Jewish authorities had permission to carry out and did indeed exercise. There would be no reason to hand over the culprit to another authority.

Does John's Gospel help us here? Oddly enough (given that much of John is clearly much more removed from gritty reality than the Synoptics), John's account of the events leading up to the trial is much more plausible, and has led many commentators to believe that the author was indeed '[the disciple] whom Jesus loved' (John 13:23). John puts the Last Supper and the crucifixion a day earlier, so that the meal and the arrest are not in the holy time of Passover. His 'trial' narrative is also very different: no meeting of the 71 members of the Sanhedrin, but instead two encounters with the key individuals who bridged between Jews and Romans – Annas, former high priest, and Caiaphas, current high priest and son-in-law of Annas – and whose role required them to keep the peace (John 18:13, 24). At these encounters there is no mention of blasphemy: Jesus is simply passed like a parcel from Annas, who binds him, to Caiaphas, and on to Pilate.

Pilate comes out and asks the Jews (who to avoid impurity on the eve of the Passover may not enter the Praetorium) what is the charge, and again they make no mention of blasphemy, but instead accuse Jesus of being 'a criminal'.[25]

The account in John gets us off a number of hooks. However, John follows the Synoptics in depicting Pilate as a benevolent man forced by the Jews to have Jesus crucified; and he, like them, reports the story of the mob choosing Barabbas over Jesus. The option to make a choice is not reported elsewhere, but we could allow it as a one-off. A more serious problem is the way Pilate is described. Vermes in particular questions the picture painted by the Synoptics and by John of Pontius Pilate as a thoughtful, inquiring judge whose reluctance to convict Jesus is such a feature of the narrative. Vermes points out that this is certainly not the Pilate of history, a governor renowned – even by Roman standards – for his high-handed and insensitive treatment of the Jews and for his random brutality. Both Josephus and Tacitus single out Pilate as deliberately provocative to the Jews, and Philo writing around 41 AD speaks of Pilate's 'vindictiveness and furious temper' and describes him as 'naturally inflexible, a blend of self-will and relentlessness', a man whose conduct as governor was characterised by 'briberies, insults, robberies, outrages and wanton injuries, executions without trial constantly repeated, ceaseless and supremely grievous cruelty'. Indeed Josephus records that Pilate handed out so many beatings and crucifixions that in 37 AD he was recalled to Rome, forced to account for his behaviour, and moved to another post.

Behind all these doubts about Pilate is a yet more serious challenge: would Jesus, seen by the Romans as a minor figure in a long line of Jewish fanatics, have come before Pilate at all? Crucifixion was a commonplace punishment for any kind of political offence; Jesus had been arrested by a small group of soldiers or temple guards and was not a mighty warlord or a serious military challenge; there would have been many hapless men awaiting execution on that morning, and no reason why Jesus should have been singled out even to see Pilate, let alone for the most important man in Jerusalem (and one known as a violent bully) to spend a substantial part of his busy morning trying to reverse the sentence of a minor political prisoner. If John's account is right, unofficial condemnation by Annas and Caiaphas would have been perfectly adequate for Pilate: he knew that they were ready to work closely and pragmatically with the Roman authorities and were as keen as he was to avoid trouble at Passover ('Now Caiaphas was he, which gave counsel to the Jews, that it was expedient that one man should die for the people', John 18:14). As Reza Aslan brutally but honestly puts it, 'Jesus was executed by the Roman state for the crime of sedition … one can dismiss the theatrical trial before Pilate as pure fantasy'.[26]

So where does this leave us? We can finish with five conclusions.

a)   What the Synoptics say about the trial cannot be squared with what John says. Both cannot be true.

b) The Synoptics' account of the trial in front of the Sanhedrin on the Passover morning is impossible on grounds of timing, of procedure, and of content.

c) Though it does not fit with the accounts in the other three Gospels, John's account of the same events up till the meeting with Pilate is more plausible.

d) The account of Pilate's behaviour in all four Gospels is so out of character that it cannot be taken seriously.

e) There is good reason to doubt whether Jesus ever came before Pilate at all.

The trial of Jesus, as presented by all four evangelists, is one of the most extraordinary, dramatic, and moving stories ever written. But that does not make it true.

How long did the Gospel writers expect that the world would last?

Bible critics trying to sift the original wheat from the subsequent chaff have come up with a wonderful phrase: the criterion of embarrassment. This refers to parts of the Gospel that Christians wish weren't there – items that are simply embarrassing. The early Church would have loved to airbrush out of history the fact that John the Baptist baptised Jesus, suggesting that Jesus required the blessing of John and not the other way round; that Jesus came from Galilee; that he kept very disreputable company in the shape of publicans, sinners, and fallen women ('publicans' were Jews who collected tax on behalf of the Roman government, thus collaborating with the enemy to oppress their own people); that he repeatedly affirmed that his message was to Jews and not to Gentiles; that the future apostle Paul was part of the mob that killed Stephen, the first Christian martyr. Worse still, the Church had to cope with Jesus being conceived out of wedlock, and killed on a cross. How do we know that these are 'facts'? Well, they are certainly embarrassing, which suggests that if the Church did include them, it is probably because it had to – because they were too widely known to be glossed over – rather than because it wanted to. Their very inconsistency with other elements of the Bible makes them more, rather than less credible.

All three Synoptics, and many of the writers of the Epistles, stated that the world would end, and Jesus come again, within their own lifetime. All the evidence is that Jesus believed this too. This is also somewhat embarrassing!

The belief in an approaching end is made clear by Jesus himself in the Gospels. From his opening proclamation at the very start of his preaching ('The time is fulfilled, and the kingdom of God is at hand', Mark 1:15), right through to his final preaching in Jerusalem, he is consistent that the last days are at hand.* This

---

* 'For the elect's sake, whom he hath chosen, he hath shortened the days' (Mark 13:20); 'Verily I say unto you, that this generation shall not pass, till all these things [that is, the last days of the world] be done' (Mark 13:30; see also Matthew 24:34, and Luke 21:32); 'Verily I say unto you, There be some standing here, which shall not taste of death, till they see the Son of Man coming in his kingdom' (Matthew 16:28, Mark 9:1, Luke 9:27).

is particularly pointed in the Last Supper: 'But I say unto you, I will not drink henceforth of this fruit of the vine, until that day when I drink it new with you in my Father's kingdom' (Matthew 26:29, Mark 14:25, Luke 22:18). If we are to take the Gospel in any way as a historical record, we cannot get away from the fact that Jesus believed in the imminent arrival of the Kingdom of God on earth.

This belief gives to the Gospels (particularly to Mark) and to the Epistles (particularly those written by Paul) their characteristic urgency and pace. The writers are men in a hurry, as shown by their simple and unadorned style, without time for fancy phrasing and fine words. Disciples should avoid all earthly commitments because the world will not last long enough to fulfil them. There is no time to lose! Don't get distracted! Don't waste time getting married or burying the dead! Don't mess around making money! Live righteously! Watch and wake! Like Boy Scouts, it was the duty of Christians to be prepared, for the end could come at any time.

The same faith in the imminent and triumphant return of Jesus is also confidently stated by Paul in his Letters, written from the 40s AD onwards: 'The time is short ... the fashion [form] of this world passeth away ... The night is far spent, the day is at hand' (1 Corinthians 7:29 and 31, Romans 13:12. See also Romans 16:20 and Philippians 4:5). So keen is the anticipation that Paul in his very first letter finds himself in difficulty trying to explain why some of the faithful had been allowed to die before the return of Jesus (1 Thessalonians 4:13–18).

Even the Epistle of James, probably written down by a follower in the 80s from sermons delivered before James was martyred in 62 AD, shows the same faith and the same urgency: 'Be ye also patient; stablish your hearts; for the coming of the Lord draweth nigh. Grudge not one against another, brethren, lest ye be condemned: behold, the judge standeth before the door' (James 5:8–9).

Not to put too fine a point on it, the writers of the Synoptic Gospels were wrong. And if they were wrong – so was Jesus.

Did St Paul invent Christianity?

St Paul played such an important role in the spread of the early Church that we can pretty safely say that Christianity would not exist without him. But did he follow Christ's teaching – or invent it?

The story of Paul's life is extensively recounted in Acts, where we are told that he was born as Saul in Tarsus, now part of Turkey. According to Acts, he became a Pharisee, a group of intense, thoughtful readers and practitioners of the Torah. At some point he moved to Jerusalem to study under the Jewish teacher Gamaliel and we first hear of him only months after the death of Jesus, at the stoning of the first Christian martyr Stephen: 'and the witnesses laid down their clothes at a young man's feet, whose name was Saul' (Acts 7:58). Saul then starts to persecute the members of the early Church (8:3) and asks permission to take the fight to Damascus (9:1–2). On the way, Acts recounts how Saul undergoes the famous 'road to Damascus' experience: 'And suddenly there shined round about him a light from heaven: And he fell to the earth, and heard a voice saying unto him, "Saul, Saul, why persecutest thou me?"' (9:3–4). Saul arises blind. Led into Damascus, he is healed by the disciple Ananias and – now renamed (Acts 13:9) with the Greek name of Paul, or 'the little one' – starts an equally energetic programme of promoting and spreading the Christian faith he had formerly so opposed.

This would be remarkable in itself, but Paul's contribution to Christianity is only just starting. His letters (it is thought that at least seven of the 21 are wholly or partly by him)* are the earliest statement of the beliefs and practices that guided the early Church, written at a time when there was no such thing as 'orthodoxy' and when it was becoming essential to set out a core set of values both to standardise the different centres of the new faith, and to set it off from paganism on the one hand, and the faith of the Jews on the other. Paul died in Rome at some point in the mid-60s AD: at the time of his death not a single one of the Gospels we have now had been written.

And there is something much more important than that. As we shall see, it seems likely that Jesus saw his mission as uniquely to Jews. Paul, after much reflection and some intellectual gymnastics, felt that the approaching end of the world

---

* 1 Thessalonians, Galatians, 1 Corinthians, Philippians, Philemon, 2 Corinthians, and Romans, probably in that order. Many scholars think that Colossians and 2 Thessalonians are also by him.

required a mission to the Gentiles also – and he saw himself as the man to conduct that mission. There were Jewish communities, one being in Paul's birthplace Tarsus, right around the Mediterranean, and many Gentiles attended the weekly services in the synagogue. According to Acts, Paul set out to convert the Jews of the Diaspora, but did not turn away Gentiles, and Acts records time and again that the Gentiles of these cities were more responsive to his message than the Jews. Paul developed a complex theology of his own to justify this, which we need not concern ourselves with now. What is crucial is that by 60 AD, there were more Christians outside Palestine than in Palestine – and even more strikingly, *more Gentile Christians than Jewish Christians*. Why does this matter? Well, when the Romans responded to the Jewish bid for independence by flattening the Temple and the city of Jerusalem in 70 AD, they effectively wiped out the community of Jewish Christians centred on the Temple. Only the converts outside Palestine – overwhelmingly Gentile – were left.

So it is not far-fetched to call Paul the founder of Christianity: founder of much of its faith (notably the doctrine of the atonement), and founder of the early churches – in Syria, in Turkey, in Greece, and above all in Rome – that took on the faith in Jesus as Christ, anointed Saviour, and preserved it for future generations. If Paul had not firmly installed the religion of Christ in the world outside Palestine, there would not be a Christian Church in the world today.

Few would challenge that judgement, or deny Paul the respect that he deserves. He was an extraordinary man, very persuasive, highly original, and completely fearless. But like many remarkable men, he was not troubled by self-doubt. Before we accept uncritically everything he said, we should look closely at the evidence in the New Testament.

The first thing to say is that most people learn about Paul from Acts, written by the author of Luke. Unfortunately, as Paula Fredriksen puts it, 'what little biographical information Paul does give us seems to fatally compromise, if not contradict, what we have from Luke'.[27] Acts recounts that Paul studied in Jerusalem, actively persecuted the early followers of Christ in that city, and went straight back there to preach the Gospel after his conversion on the Damascus road. It further adds that he took the Gospel to the Gentiles only after his attempts to bring it to the Diaspora Jews had been rejected. Paul, on the other hand, says nothing of studying in Jerusalem, never mentions leading 'persecutions' there, and claims that after his conversion, rather than returning to Jerusalem, he moved to Arabia and then to Damascus – indeed, that three years after his conversion he was still 'unknown by face' to the churches of Judea (Galatians 1:13–24). Moreover he claims that he set out from the start to take the word to the Gentiles.

A notable example of the mismatch with Acts is the fact that in all his writings, Paul never once mentions the famous 'road to Damascus' conversion that is such a major and well known feature of Luke's account!

The most likely explanation for this is also the simplest, namely that Luke, the author of Acts, writing 30 years or more after Paul's death and 40 or 50 years after Paul wrote his letters, did not know of the existence of those letters, and had only idealised stories and hazy recollections to go on. At the time Luke wrote Acts (90–100 AD), each of Paul's letters rested with its destination church: only later were they shared and collated. Just as Luke in his Gospel created a beautiful fiction to explain and contextualise the birth of Jesus, so Luke created in Acts a beautiful fiction to dramatise the thrilling exploits of Paul, the hero who took the faith of Jesus to the Gentiles and began the process of bringing Christianity to the Roman Empire.

So let us assume that Acts is in this respect at least a work of the imagination, and take our information directly from Paul himself as recorded in his Letters. My point here is not to enter a theological debate, but to point out how very personal Paul's beliefs are – to the extent that they cannot in any way be derived from the Gospel accounts of what Jesus said and did. Very briefly, Paul believed that Jesus existed before the creation of the world (Philippians 2:6ff, 1 Corinthians 2:7 and 8:9, Galatians 4:4, Romans 8:3), that he came down from heaven to save the world, that his death on the cross redeemed us all (Jew and Gentile alike) from our sins, that when he returned – and Paul expected that to happen within his lifetime – we would all be resurrected with new and glorious bodies (1 Corinthians 15:51–52), and that there would be a final and stupendous battle, led by Jesus, against the massed forces of evil, in which good would triumph and usher in the reign of God.

If these seem familiar ideas, it is because they are just that; they have formed the backbone of Christianity since it was codified in the 4th and 5th centuries AD. Paul constantly asserts (for example Romans 1:2) that they were foretold in the Scriptures as well as communicated to him by Jesus. But as we have seen, there is nothing in the Old Testament, and very little in the New, to give any basis for these splendid inventions. Did Paul then make them up himself? We have to say that on the evidence we have, he did indeed, and quite unashamedly, carve out his own faith in glorious isolation. That isolation was not a necessity: had he gone to Jerusalem he could have consulted, not only the disciples of Jesus, but even the members of Jesus' family – members who were the core of the Jerusalem church. James, the brother of Jesus, was the head of the Jerusalem church and almost certainly the author of the Epistle that bears his name. But Paul had no interest in this group. By his own account, he did not get in touch with them till three years after his conversion; he set off on his preaching tour without 'doing his time' in Palestine; he never anchors his theology by any references to those who knew Jesus.

And why should he? He refers to himself (Galatians 1:1, 1 Corinthians 9:1) as 'an apostle' (that is, as one who is the equal of the Twelve), and as one who 'neither received [the gospel] of man … but by the revelation of Jesus Christ' (Galatians 1: 11–12). Even more, he was set apart by God before he was born, and God revealed his son directly to him, meaning that it was not necessary for him to 'confer with flesh and blood' (Galatians 1: 15–16). In 2 Corinthians 11:5 and 22–23, Paul says that he is actually a better apostle than any of the others; as Reza Aslan puts it, 'Paul does not consider himself the *thirteenth* apostle. He thinks he is the *first* apostle'.[28]

So Paul is free to create his own theology. What of the competition? He is not impressed. He is surprisingly and consistently rude about Peter, that 'rock' on which Jesus was supposedly to build his church, referring to him as 'to be blamed' and as a dissembler (Galatians 2:11 and 13). It is clear that Paul returned to Jerusalem around 50 AD to explain his teaching to the Jerusalem community. Luke gives a bland and harmonious account of this visit (Acts 15); by contrast, Paul's account at the start of Galatians refers to 'false brethren unawares [secretly] brought in, who came in privily to spy out our liberty', assures his readers that he did not give in to them, 'no, not for an hour', and describes James and Peter as supposed leaders who in fact 'added nothing to me' (Galatians 2: 5–6). It is noteworthy that almost immediately after this meeting, the Jerusalem community started sending its own missionaries to the congregations that Paul had converted in order to correct Paul's erroneous teachings; Paul's subsequent writings are full of attempts to defend himself, his status, and his teachings against these 'false apostles, deceitful workers, transforming themselves into the apostles of Christ' whom he compares to Satan (2 Corinthians 11:13–15).

In the end Paul received a summons from Jerusalem about 57 AD that he could not refuse, and as recounted in Acts 21,

he was forced by the real apostles to show his Jewish orthodoxy by submitting to a rite of purification in the Temple.
In the early 60s Paul made his way to Rome to preach his
message in the heart of the empire, but even Luke has to admit
that he was not well received by the Jewish community there
(Acts 28:25–28). This was probably because Peter was already
there and had warned them off Paul. Tellingly, Paul's letters
make no mention of these humiliations!

What does all this tell us about the man who in effect
founded the faith that is now called Christianity?

First, we know, from their behaviour over the 30 years
after Jesus' death, that the original apostles believed their mission was to Jews rather than to Gentiles. Paul's Gentile mission
was very much his own invention – as shown by the discom-
fort and opposition it aroused in those who were related to,
or had known, Jesus.

Second, it shows the bitterness between Peter and Paul –
supposedly twin pillars of the early Church.

Third, we find once again that it is impossible to accept
New Testament writings as authoritative: Acts and the Letters
of Paul contradict each other both in faith and in fact.

And fourth, we see that the theology that underpins all
subsequent Christianity is primarily the creation of a man
who had never known Jesus; who kept himself separate
from those who had, and took pains not to enquire about
their views; and who felt himself a better minister of Christ
(2 Corinthians 11:5 and 23) than the twelve apostles that Jesus
himself had chosen.

4. The New Testament as morality: what morality (and what theology) does the New Testament teach?

It is very common to hear people speak of 'Christian values', 'Christian ethics', or – on the other side of the coin – 'un-Christian behaviour'. And although we often speak of Judaeo-Christian values and traditions as though they were consistent and uniform, not surprisingly it is the New Testament rather than the Old that is seen not only as the core element, but often as superseding the Old, with a contrast between the supposedly rule-governed and vengeful religion of the Old Testament, and the forgiving spirit of the New Testament where what matters is the inner state, not the outer observance.

So let us ask – what are 'Christian values'? What morality does the New Testament teach?

First, is the New Testament offered to all the peoples of the world – or only to Jews?

We find many assurances in the Gospels that the mission is to all men (and of course women too). All three Synoptics end with the risen Jesus sending his disciples out to 'all nations' (Matthew 28:19, Mark 16:15, Luke 24:47). Paul never weakens in his determination to take the word to Gentiles, and his theology is carefully worked out to explain how this fulfils the divine plan (see Acts 10 and 11, and in due course Romans, especially Chapter 11). Conversely the treatment of Jews in the New Testament – as we have seen – is relentlessly negative.

Yet we cannot avoid a great deal of contradictory evidence. Paul's letters record a struggle in him, a conflict reflected in Acts 11:19–20: 'Now they which were scattered abroad ... [preached] the word to none but unto the Jews only. And some ... spake unto the Grecians, preaching the Lord Jesus.' Those who preached only to Jews had reasons for their actions. Whatever changes his later followers made, the evidence is overwhelming of 'a firm tradition that Jesus had not ordered a mission to the Gentiles',[29] and that Jesus thought of his mission as being entirely to his own people. Consider, for example, the reluctance to heal a Syrophoenician child ('It is not meet to take the children's bread, and to cast it to dogs', Matthew 15:26, Mark 7:27: bread represents healing that belongs by right to the children of God, that is the Jews, and not to the non-Jewish Syrophoenicians). Consider too the limitation placed upon the twelve apostles to 'Go not into the way of the Gentiles ... but go rather to the lost sheep of the house of Israel' (Matthew 10:5–6 and 15:24), and the promise to those apostles that they will 'judge the twelve tribes of Israel' (Matthew 19:28, Luke 22:30). And the very early Church, as we know from Acts and the Letters, did indeed keep itself in Jerusalem and regard the Temple as 'head office': the principal leaders of the movement – the apostles Peter and John, and Jesus' brother James – maintained their fealty to Jewish customs and Mosaic Law until the end. Jesus' insistence on the primacy of Jewish Law (Matthew 5:17) and his desire to focus on the lost sheep of the house of Israel – embarrassing as this became after his death – cannot be sidestepped.

Second, is the morality of the New Testament forgiving – or punitive? There is the morality of this world – and the morality of the next. All cultures wonder whether there is a life after death. The Romans speculated about a rather dreary afterlife populated by shadowy forms of the living, and the Jews of the Old Testament period had Sheol, the realm of the dead, but it was not a pillar of their faith. We saw in Part One of this book that the Old Testament religion of the Hebrews was very much about this world and its redemption, rather than about an afterlife, and this carries through to the period in which the events of the New Testament took place: by and large the Jews of Jesus' time believed that life ended with death. (The fact that the Pharisees were mentioned as believing in an afterlife merely reinforces the point that the vast majority of their fellow-believers didn't.)

Into this world the writings of the New Testament burst like a bomb. There is an afterlife: it is eternal: and it is joyful. But who is it for? Is God punitive – or loving? Will justice prevail – or mercy? Will everyone be saved – or only the righteous?

Christian theology has been uncompromising. Catholics, drawing on Matthew 25:31–46, believe that there is a Last Judgement, at which some are allocated to Hell (a place of permanent torment), some to Purgatory (where they are 'purged' of their sins before being saved), and some directly to Heaven. (Modifying Matthew's teaching, they assert that only christened believers go to Heaven.) Protestants did not challenge the Last Judgement; they took out Purgatory, but kept Hell. The threat of damnation runs through the whole of the New Testament: not only in Matthew, but in Mark ('it is better for thee to enter into life maimed, than having two hands to go into hell', Mark 9:43); in Luke's parable of Dives and Lazarus (Luke 16:19–31); and in John ('And shall come forth [from their graves]; they that have done good, unto the resurrection of life; and they that have done evil, unto the resurrection of damnation', John 5:29). It goes on into the Letters of Paul ('Behold therefore the goodness and severity of God: on them which fell, severity; but toward thee, goodness, if thou continue in his goodness: otherwise thou also shalt be cut off' (Romans 11:22)), and the Letter of James: 'Go to now, ye rich men, weep and howl for your miseries that shall come upon you' (James 5:1). And of course the Revelation of St John has a splendid list of those who will suffer for ever in the lake of burning brimstone: 'the fearful, and unbelieving, and the abominable, and murderers, and whoremongers, and sorcerers, and idolaters, and all liars' (Revelation 21:8).

For well over a thousand years this interpretation of Scripture guided the theology of the Church and determined its behaviour towards heretics and sinners. If the sinner – or the unbeliever – is damned, then simple charity requires us to save that sinner from damnation: no penalty, and no torture, in this world, can ever be as awful as the torture that awaits in the next.

But what if the sinner is *not* damned?

There is a growing strand of Bible scholarship that points to a different teaching: one in which divine love is not selective, but universal, and in which there is no room for damnation. We find this in Revelation ('And God shall wipe away all tears from their eyes; and there shall be no more death, neither sorrow, nor crying, neither shall there be any more pain', 21:4). And we find it in the writings of Paul: 'For as in Adam all die, *even so in Christ shall all be made alive*' (1 Corinthians 15–22, italics added); 'even so by the right-eousness of one *the free gift came upon all men unto justification of life*' (Romans 5:18, italics added; see also Romans 11:32 and Colossians 1:19–20). But then Revelation is a very late text, and you can find most things in Paul if you know where to look. What about the Gospels, where we have a chance of getting closer to the authentic words of Jesus? We have seen the case the Gospels make for a Last Judgement and an eternity of damnation. But is that the only view they give us of the nature of God?

I think not. If there is a stern, judgemental, selective Jesus – and there certainly is – there is also a mild, forgiving, inclusive Jesus. This is the Jesus who calls his heavenly father 'Abba' – Dad – and who paints that father as infinitely for-giving and generous. 'Ask and it shall be given you; seek, and ye shall find … What man is there of you, whom if his son ask bread, will he give him a stone?' (Matthew 7:7–9). This is the Jesus who urges his followers to forgive, not seven times, but seventy times seven (Matthew 18:22), or as Luke puts it, 'Love your enemies, do good to those which hate you, bless them that curse you, and pray for them which despitefully use you' (Luke 6:27–28). This is the Jesus who even on the cross asks that his persecutors be forgiven (Luke 23:34). And this is the Jesus whose follower Paul created in 1 Corinthians 13 and Romans 8:38–39 two of the most celebrated hymns ever written to love and to a loving God.

Which is the real Jesus? Indeed, which is the real God? Who knows – but what we do know is that the New Testament offers us both, *and they can't both be true.*

Thirdly, is the message of the New Testament one of conformity, obedience, and propriety – or was Jesus frankly a dissenter and a rebel? What would he have thought of respectability?

The established churches that we know in the modern world are profoundly – well, establishment: forces for law and order, for conformity and respectability, for monogamous marriage and the traditional family with a clearly defined hierarchy for husband, wife, and children. Their sacraments of baptism, marriage, and burial, like the Sunday morning service followed by the Sunday roast, are all part of the ordered life of society. In this they follow closely the advice of Peter, Paul, and James to the early Church. The first Christians required believers to live in settled communities of blameless respectability, supporting themselves in regular employment ('We commanded you, that if any would not work, neither should he eat', 2 Thessalonians 3:10) and led by worthy deacons of quite exceptional dullness (1 Timothy 3:1–12).

By contrast, the Gospels constantly and amazingly emphasise the irresponsible, imprudent, joyful, and deeply 'un-sensible' side of Jesus. This is the man who wanders round

Galilee with no wife, no children, and no visible means of support except the savings of the women who follow him (Luke 8:3); who calls on his followers to be like the lilies of the field, taking no thought for the morrow; who welcomes and consorts with tax-collectors and sinners and who eats and drinks in their houses with enthusiasm, whose contribution to a wedding (John 2:6) is to produce *over a hundred gallons* of wine, who allows a devotee to anoint him with a jar of spikenard 'which might have been sold ... and given to the poor' (Mark 14:5), who orders his disciples to go out into the cities of Galilee with neither food nor money and to live off charity. This is the Jesus who allows Martha to slave away washing dishes in the kitchen so that her sister Mary can sit in the front room and talk to him about the meaning of life (Luke 10:38–42). This is a man who consistently values freedom over control; impulse over reflection; desire over restraint; paradox over reason; wit over effort; and joy over work. Anything less sensible and respectable (and more calculated to irritate an average Sunday-morning congregation) would be hard to imagine!

For those branches of Christianity – and that includes most – that put the family at the centre of their faith and worship, Jesus must be a constant disappointment. This is not just because of his refusal to penalise the woman taken in adultery (John 8:1–11), or his insistence that his followers abandon their domestic bonds and familial responsibilities to follow him (for example Luke 9:60). It is not just because he himself appears to have had neither wife nor children – or, if he did have them, to have abandoned them so absolutely that they make no appearance in the official records. As much as anything it is because when Jesus comes to speak directly about families and communities, he is so off-hand about them. His return to Nazareth is a disaster, revealing that he could do no great works among those who knew him as a child and young man, and prompting the famous comment that 'a prophet is not without honour, but in his own country' (Matthew 13:57, Mark 6:4, Luke 4:24). His attitude to his family of origin – if the Gospels are to be believed – is similarly dismissive: when they send word to him through the press of his followers, he responds with the cutting comment, 'Who is my mother, or my brethren?' (Mark 3:33).

If Jesus is financially irresponsible and indifferent to family values – the kind of foreign immigrant you would certainly reject if he applied for UK citizenship – what about his politics? Here again the peaceful, conservative, conformist picture painted by the established churches since the 1st century AD seems starkly undermined by the Gospel accounts. If the Sermon on the Mount is to be believed, it is the poor, the downtrodden, the losers who are blessed: wealth – as in the story of Dives and Lazarus (Luke 16:19–31) – leads directly to damnation.

And should his followers accept this world of injustice, of poverty, of oppression? Is this a religion of resignation – or of action? Of compliance – or of rebellion? Well, there is plenty of evidence for the compliant, other-worldly Jesus whose kingdom is 'not of this world' and who advocates 'turning the other cheek'. But let us not forget the references in the Synoptics to violent division: 'Think not that I am come to send peace on earth: I came not to send peace, but a sword' (Matthew 10:34); the peculiar comment in Luke's Last Supper (Luke 22:36–38) that it is time for selling cloaks and buying swords; and above all consider the manner of Jesus' death. He was crucified (the death meted out to political rebels) in between two 'lestai' (bandits), and with his crime – 'King of the Jews' – clearly defined by the Romans as political.

We asked earlier – questioning whether Jesus was forgiving or punitive – 'Which is the real Jesus?'. And at this point we need to return to that question. Orthodox Christianity sees here a paradox, but not a problem: Jesus is the Son of God, born without physical intercourse as a unique combination of God and man, an example to all of us of the perfect human life lived without sin, risen from the grave as a physical body, the Saviour who with his willingly accepted death takes over the burden of guilt from all of us, redeems us all from our sins, and points us to a divine kingdom that is 'not of this world'.

Did the Gospel writers see him in this way?

It seems unlikely that they did. If we could speak to the author of Mark, writing a generation after the crucifixion, we would find that he attached little importance to the idea that Jesus died as a sacrifice for the sins of humanity (there are only two references in Mark to this, 10:45 and 14:24; scholars suspect that both are later additions). We would find a Jesus who though certainly 'a' son of God – a righteous man – never seems to think of himself as 'the' Son of God; a Jesus who never describes himself, or is described, as of sacred birth; who dies in despair (Mark 15:34); and whose followers are left at the end baffled and frightened. The original ending of Mark (16:8) is scarcely a triumphant one: 'neither said they any thing to any man, for they were afraid'.

'Son of God'

'Son of God' is a much misunderstood phrase and needs some explanation. The New Testament writers used the Greek phrase 'huios theou', which has parallels in Greek mythology where the gods actually fathered children. But it is much more likely that this was simply a translation of a Hebrew or Aramaic phrase used in both Old and New Testaments, which had a very different meaning. The terms 'sons of God' and 'son of God' appear frequently in Jewish literature, and leaders of the people, kings and princes were called 'sons of God'. In the Old Testament its primary meaning was 'just man' or 'one favoured by God': in Psalm 2:7, God addresses David with the words, 'Thou art my Son: this day have I begotten thee'. This carries over to the New Testament, as in John: 'as many as received him, to them gave he power to become the sons of God' (John 1:12), in 1 John 3:1-2, or in Galatians 3:26 ('ye are all the children of God by faith in Christ Jesus'). There is no suggestion of sacred birth or physical paternity there.

Above all – as we saw earlier – we would find a very this-worldly Jesus who believed in the imminent arrival of the Kingdom of God.

So how do we begin to understand and make sense of these contradictions in story and in morality?

5. The historical context (continued): the events of the 1st century AD, the world in which Jesus lived (4 BC to the early 30s AD) and the New Testament was written

As we saw above, Judea at the time of the birth of Jesus was a turbulent country full of 'messianic expectations'. This ferment continued throughout the life of Jesus. Contemporary historians list rebellions led by prophets and messiahs such as Hezekiah the bandit chief, Simon of Peraea, Athronges the Shepherd, and Judas the Galilean around the turn of the century, and the New Testament itself refers to 'that Egyptian, which before these days madest an uproar, and leddest out into the wilderness four thousand men' (Acts 21:38). After Jesus' death 'the Samaritan' gathered a group of followers in 36 AD, in 44 Theudas the prophet attracted huge crowds to the River Jordan, and in 46 two sons of Judas the Galilean launched a revolutionary movement to overturn Roman rule.

All were hunted down and killed by the Roman authorities.

In the following years rebellion seems to have given way to terrorism. Initially the principal victims were not the Roman occupiers but the Jewish priestly aristocracy who collaborated with the occupiers. The main target was the High Priest Jonathan, and in 56 AD, during the Passover celebrations, a *sicarius* (daggerman) stepped out of the crowd and cut the high priest's throat in broad daylight, vanishing back into the crowd. Emboldened by this feat the *sicarii* ramped up their campaign and launched a reign of terror so severe that Josephus wrote: 'More terrible than their crimes was the fear they aroused, every man hourly expecting death, as in war.'[30]

It is important to understand the motivation of the *sicarii*. Like the jihadis of our own time, they robbed, stole, kidnapped, and murdered. But it was a jihad: a religious campaign, a crusade, to rid the Holy Land, not only of its alien occupiers, but also of all, even co-religionists, who offended against purity and justice. And their slogan was as simple and uncompromising as that of any jihadi: 'No lord but God!'

Jewish resistance and brutal Roman reprisals escalated to the point where in 66 AD a loose alliance of Jewish 'freedom fighters' attacked and killed the Roman garrison in Jerusalem and in effect declared independence. In 68 Vespasian, the Roman emperor, sent his son Titus to recapture the city. The ensuing siege was bitter and absolutely ruthless, a showcase for Roman power and a warning to the whole empire of the dangers of rebellion. Those who attempted to escape from the city were crucified in full view of the besieged, or decapitated so that their heads could be catapulted back into the city. There was only one possible outcome, and by 70 – weakened by constant and highly destructive infighting between the three Jewish groups controlling the city and the Temple

– the garrison had fallen. But the objective of the siege was not only the recapture of Jerusalem. It was the complete obliteration of the Temple as a place of worship, of Jerusalem as a city, and of Judea as a state. When Mark writes, 'Seest thou these great buildings? there shall not be left one stone upon another, that shall not be thrown down' (Mark 13:2), he is scarcely exaggerating.

When the Romans did decide to make their final push, as well as slaughtering huge numbers of the exhausted and starving survivors, they burned the whole city. The foundations of the Temple were set on fire and the entire building destroyed. The intention was to humiliate the Jewish people and remove Jerusalem from the map. The sacred treasures of the Temple, including a copy of the Torah, were taken to Rome and displayed in a triumphal procession. The Jews were forbidden to rebuild their Temple, and the two-drachma tax that all Jews – whether living in Palestine or beyond it – formerly paid to the Temple with the permission of Rome, was commuted to a tax payable to Rome: by a particular twist of humiliation, this went to the rebuilding of the Temple of Jupiter in Jerusalem, accidentally destroyed during the siege. All survivors were expelled from the city; all the country became the personal property of the Roman emperor; and by 135 AD the very names of Jerusalem and Judea were replaced on Roman maps by 'Aelia Capitolina' and 'Palestine'. To quote Martin Goodman, 'There could not be a clearer demonstration that the conquest was being celebrated, not just over Judea, but over Judaism'.[31]

The parallels with the destruction of the first Temple by the Babylonians in 587 BC are obvious. What did this second defeat mean for the people of Israel?

For the Jews of Judea this was not just a defeat. It was a crushing and overwhelming disappointment. The defeat of 587 BC was the final closing of a vice that had been tightening for 200 years. The defeat of 70 AD came at the end of 200 years of rebuilding – independence under the Hasmoneans (163–140 BC), Herod's limited self-rule under the Romans, and (as we have seen) growing apocalyptic expectations expressed through the series of visionary leaders who led rebellions throughout and after the lifetime of Jesus.

The consequence for Jews resident in Judea and Galilee was the complete transformation of the Jewish faith into what we now know as rabbinic Judaism. But that is not the subject of this book. Our focus here is the New Testament – none of which, except the Letters of Paul, had even been written down at the time of the fall of Jerusalem.* What did the crushing of the Jewish dream mean for the early Christians?

First, and overwhelmingly, it meant the end of Jewish Christianity – the faith of James the brother of Jesus, of Peter the friend and companion of Jesus, and of the surviving apostles, all of whom had remained in Jerusalem preaching to Jews,

---

* It is fair to say that the hypothetical 'Q' source (see page 149) that forms significant parts of Matthew and Luke was already in circulation by this time. However, we can say with confidence that no trace of the actual Q has yet been found.

praying in the Temple, and following the Torah. From the crucifixion through to the fall of Jerusalem, the headquarters of the faith was in the Temple: Jewish Christians – or more accurately Christian Jews – were accepted and respected by the Temple hierarchy. In 62 AD James, head of the Christian Church in Jerusalem, was executed by the High Priest Ananus. The result was an outcry among Jews, led by Pharisees, which culminated in the Romans removing Ananus from office.

Until 70 AD, Jerusalem was the mother church. After 70, it was a liability.

What happened to the members of the Jerusalem community? We shall never know for sure. We know from Justin Martyr and Irenaeus, 2nd-century Christian writers, of a Jewish group who 'believe in Christ, keep the Law, and induce Gentile Christians to do so'.[32] Significantly, given the crucial importance of the poor in both Old and New Testaments, this group is referred to as 'Ebionites' (from a Hebrew word meaning 'poor'). By the end of the century this group, holding to the Torah and refusing to accept the virgin birth of Jesus, had been condemned as heretics, and no more is heard of them.

But in relation to the first Jewish Christians, the Jerusalem community of 33–70 AD, the family, friends, and converts who had in many cases actually known Jesus, it is tempting to make a connection with a passing remark in Josephus, who was himself one of the besieged and spoke as an eye-witness. In his description of the final moments of the city he mentions a group of 6,000 who as the Roman soldiers closed around them, gathered on the last colonnade of the ruined Temple 'to receive the signs of their deliverance'.[33] If it was indeed them, they had lived for their faith; and in the footsteps of their leader, they died for it.

The end of the dominance of Jerusalem – the destruction of the mother church – enabled Christianity to cut itself away from its Jewish roots. The most obvious, dramatic, and frequently overlooked demonstration of this reframed religion stares us in the face. The language of Judaism and the Old Testament was Hebrew. The language of Jesus, his family, his friends, and his followers, was Aramaic. *But the language of the Gospels is Greek.*

We know that from the earliest days there were 'Hebrews' and 'Hellenists' among the disciples and that there was rivalry between them (see Acts 6:1, but also the whole question already discussed of the relation between Paul on the one hand, and Peter and James on the other). The use of Greek was a decisive abandonment of the Hebrew tradition, and of the Aramaic language in which Gabriel spoke to Mary, in which the angels sang to the shepherds, and in which Jesus preached, prayed, and finally made his last cry on the cross. It was a huge victory for Hellenists over Hebrews.

Why such a decisive shift? For two, connected, reasons. First, the writers of the Gospel were not from the Jerusalem community. Of course they weren't: the Jerusalem community, the Hebrews, didn't exist any more, and in any case it is pretty likely that the members of that community were largely or wholly unlettered. But even more importantly, the writers of the Gospel weren't writing for Jews in Palestine

– the ones, like Jesus, who spoke Aramaic. They were writing for Diaspora Jews, the expatriate Jewish population scattered around the cities of the Mediterranean. They had turned their attention from Judea – the losers – to the Roman Empire, where the real power lay.

The Diaspora (significantly, the word is Greek) was not new: there was a community on Elephant Island in the Nile as early as the 8th century BC. But it vastly increased in scale after 500 BC, and by the birth of Jesus there were Jewish communities all over the Mediterranean. It is remarkable to realise that by the time of Jesus, just as in our own times, there were more Jews living outside Judea than within it. These communities kept the Torah and their sense of their own identity, faith, and customs: but increasingly Greek, rather than Hebrew, was their first language – hence the creation of the Greek Bible, the Septuagint, both by and for these Hellenised Jewish communities. They needed somewhere to worship, which gave rise to Greek-speaking synagogues. And because there was something distinctive about Jewish faith and practice in comparison with the other religions of the Classical world, many Gentiles (non-Jews) came to attend services and take instruction, spreading awareness of the Torah outwards into the non-Jewish world.

The language of these Diaspora Jews was *koine* (general-purpose) Greek. And it was also (rather bizarrely) the language of the Roman Empire. The shift of audience from Jews to Romans brought with it some uncomfortable conse-quences. It is impossible to escape the fact that all four Gospels

– and every reference in the Epistles – agree that Jesus was crucified, in other words sentenced by a Roman authority (the Jews did not have the right to carry out that punishment) to a Roman form of execution. This is awkward, indeed embarrassing, if you are trying to appeal to a Roman readership. Who are you to blame? If Jesus is the victim, who is the perpetrator?

The strategy adopted in Mark, and refined in the later Gospels, is of course to blame 'the Jews'. Given that Jesus and his disciples were all Jews (as Mark may have been also), this is somewhat contradictory, but it is achieved by sleight of hand. Initially Jesus is seen as proposing a simple, universal, inclusive kind of Judaism – one that is opposed by a complex, selective, exclusive approach to the faith attributed to 'the scribes and Pharisees'. When Jesus moves his campaign from Galilee to Jerusalem, his inclusive creed enables him to appeal to the simple pilgrims – but arouses the suspicion and opposition of the Jerusalem establishment, ultimately represented by the High Priest Caiaphas. So for much of the Gospels the condemnation of 'the Jews' is intended to refer, not to the rural poor of Galilee, but to the educated, wealthy, powerful, and metropolitan classes of Jerusalem. In that sense Jesus is a kind of Robin Hood figure, a romantic anti-establishment dissident.

Where everything turns very nasty from our perspective in the 21st century is at Jesus' trial. Here, instead of polarising priestly establishment (bad) against common people (good), all four evangelists set Jews (bad) against Romans (good) by making the Jewish crowd force Pilate to crucify Jesus (Matthew 27:20–26, Mark 15:11–15, Luke 23:13–25,

John 18:38–40 and 19:15), culminating in the terrible cry in Matthew 27:25, 'His blood be upon us, and on our children!' The purpose, and the result, is to divert attention from the fact that it was the Romans who actually carried out the execution. John takes submissiveness to Rome even further: the chief priests assert that 'We have no king but Caesar' (John 19:15), and Jesus is actually made to say, 'He that delivered me unto thee [the high priest] hath the greater sin [than the Roman governor]' (John 19:11). The consequences for Christian anti-Semitism have been appalling.

The fall of Jerusalem does not influence politics alone. It has a huge effect on the theology of the early Church. We have seen that Jesus predicted a 'Second Coming' within the lifetime of his hearers, with the expectation that his kingdom would be installed upon earth. After the fall of Jerusalem this expectation became increasingly hard to sustain. (What is more, given the need to appeal to a Gentile population owing allegiance to the Roman emperor, the idea of the approaching kingship of Jesus on earth was clearly not one that would go down well.) From 70 AD the whole see-saw starts to shift from the kingdom of God upon earth, to the kingship of God in heaven – from this life to the afterlife – and from a political messiah to a spiritual one: a process that culminates, as we shall see, in the other-worldly Jesus of John's gospel. The enigmatic phrase that Jesus uses to Pilate, 'My kingdom is not of this world' (John 18:36), comes to represent this transformation and to head off any suggestions of an attempt by the new faith to challenge the earthly rule of Rome.

Last – but far from least – the fall of Jerusalem, the collapse of the mother church, and the extinction of Jewish hopes of the earthly triumph of a Jewish god, transformed the way the early Church viewed the theology of Paul. His self-appointed mission to the Gentiles had been seen (rightly or wrongly) as a threat to the mission to the Jews, God's chosen people. Now the mission to the Jews of Judea had been utterly crushed. What was left? When the New Testament canon was finally established in 398 AD, of the 27 books that make up the New Testament, no fewer than fourteen – thirteen Letters and Acts – were either by, attributed to, or about Paul. Paul's target audience of the Diaspora Jews and the Gentiles; Paul's theology of a pre-existent Christ whose kingdom was not of this world; Paul's attitude of prudent accommodation to the rule of Rome (he was after all a Roman citizen); Paul's vision of salvation, not through the 'works' of the Torah, but through faith in a risen Jesus; all these swept away the theology and the vision of James and the apostles, the little group of relatives and friends in Jerusalem who had known Jesus, travelled with him, heard him speak, and seen him die.

6. So – who wrote the New Testament?

We concluded the previous section with what is, or should be, a rather surprising observation: that the testimony of those who knew most about Jesus – his family, his apostles, and his companions – was completely discarded by those who carried his message forward.

We will begin this section with an equally remarkable observation: better known, yet equally regularly overlooked. However little we know about those who wrote the New Testament, we know one thing for sure. *It wasn't Jesus.*

This is more noteworthy than it may seem at first glance. If you had a compelling vision of God and man, and a startling insight into the very nature of God – wouldn't you want to ensure that it outlived you? If you were illiterate (as, for example, Mohammed was), wouldn't you do as Mohammed did, and find a scribe? And if you could neither write it yourself, nor get it written, wouldn't you put your mind to bringing together your followers and training them in your knowledge and vision?

It is very obvious – and very striking – that Jesus did none of these things. He chose followers from the Galilean poor: men of character, men of courage, but not men of scholarship. And more striking still, he did not take pains to instruct or coach them in his view of the world. If the Gospels are to be believed, he certainly passed on to some of them his miraculous healing powers even during his lifetime, and we see in Acts that some of his followers were able not only to heal, but even to match his feat of raising from the dead (Acts 20:9–12). But a recurring theme of all four Gospels is the disconnect between Jesus and his followers – his consistent exasperation with their failure to understand him. How patient was he with them? On the evidence of the evangelists, not very.

He is willing to pass on his powers: but with his knowledge he is much more cautious. A recurring theme in the

Gospels is Jesus' repeated injunction, both to his disciples and to those he heals, to 'Go, and tell no man of this'. This is so emphatic in Mark (1:23–25, 34, 43–44, 3:11–12, 5:40–43, 7:24, 32–36, 8:22–26, 30, 9:9) that a name has been coined for it, 'the messianic secret', and a whole literature has (rightly) sprung up around it. We shall return to this secrecy, but whatever the reasons for it, the outcome was to leave the field clear for others to write the story of Jesus. As we have seen, the fall of Jerusalem transformed the faith of the early Christians. And it was these post-Jerusalem believers who wrote the Gospels, Acts, and Revelation. Who were they? And how did the new direction of Christianity influence the story that they told?

We know extraordinarily little about the four evangelists, the people who wrote the first surviving accounts of Jesus. We do not know their names: the original Gospels do not bear an author's name, and Matthew, Mark, Luke, and John are all merely guesses added 50 years or more after the books were first written and circulated. We do not know where they lived (though it was almost certainly outside Judea). We do not know their sex: it is unlikely that any was a woman, but women do feature largely in all four Gospels, notably in Luke. We do not even know for sure whether the writers were Jews or Gentiles. Matthew anchors his events strongly in the Old Testament, yet it is he who makes the Jewish crowd cry, 'His blood be upon us' before the crucifixion; Luke seems to have book-knowledge of the Jewish faith but little practical knowledge of its particular rituals and beliefs (see *New Oxford Annotated Bible*, p. 1827); and John, who constantly speaks of 'the Jews' festivals', gives the impression that the writer is no more Jewish than his audience.

All this is in marked distinction to the Old Testament, and reflects a deeper contrast. By the 2nd century BC, with the publication of the Septuagint, the Old Testament had taken on a canonical status, which meant that it was forbidden to change a word of it: indeed the later Jewish copiers (the so-called Masoretes) solemnly reproduced the misprints and non sequiturs of the ancient Hebrew texts without feeling able to challenge, let alone correct, what they had inherited.

The New Testament was completely different. All four Gospels circulated in numerous versions from the earliest times and editors and copyists felt no embarrassment about amending the version they had inherited. The texts we now use, initially written between about 70 and 110 AD, were all changed, updated, added to, revised, and rewritten – not to mention copied, with all the errors that introduces – over the next century as theological opinions changed. The result is that we have no certainty as to what was the original version of our modern Gospels: textual criticism, in the old-fashioned sense of establishing an authoritative version, is highly skilled, but also extremely difficult. Any new edition of the New Testament bristles with footnotes indicating the choices that have been made between competing alternatives. As one recent writer reminds us, 'so much does the interpretation and evaluation of the manuscript evidence progress, that a new New Testament will be issued every ten or twenty years for the foreseeable future'.[34]

It is obvious that the early copyists had no belief in a 'sacred' text in the sense of a hallowed, unalterable 'vox Dei'. Rather they edited, adapted, and rewrote what they thought of as drafts, to suit their understanding and their purposes. The Masoretic copiers' sense of a text dictated by God and not to be altered under any circumstances, was in those early days completely absent.

If we know very little about the people who wrote the New Testament, what do we know about the New Testament itself?

Jesus was crucified early in the 30s. The first writings we have – the Epistles largely or wholly attributed to Paul, and possibly the Epistle of James – date from the 40s to the early 60s. (Paul is generally thought to have died in Rome in the mid-60s.) The four Gospels were written somewhere between 70 and about 95 AD: the sequence is Mark, Matthew/Luke, and finally John. They were thus begun almost two generations after Jesus' death. The remaining thirteen books of the New Testament – Revelation, Acts, and a further eleven Epistles – date from the 80s through to about 120 AD (see Appendix 2).

We have seen that there are significant differences – even major contradictions – between the four Gospels: ways in which they don't fit with each other, and ways in which they don't fit with reality. Let us look at each Gospel, and the story it tells, in the light of the historical context and circumstances at the time it was composed, and the pressing problems its author believed the early Church to be facing. Let us ask, for each Gospel: what is the question to which this Gospel is an answer?

The context of Mark's Gospel (about 70 AD)

The first Gospel in date of composition is Mark, written around 70 AD. What is the context in which Mark wrote? 'Well before Mark wrote, the mission to Israel had foundered … [the Gospel of Mark's time] was mostly proclaimed by Gentiles [to Gentiles].'[35] The world of Mark's gospel, the world of the 50s and 60s, was one in which most of the conversions were made outside Israel, and by Gentile preachers rather than by the Jerusalem-based disciples who had travelled with and learned directly from Jesus. Much of the teaching outside Israel was carried out in synagogues – because that was where 'God-fearers', Gentiles with an interest in faith, gathered; but the Jews who attended those synagogues were not well disposed to the new religion and many punishments were issued by the synagogue courts to those who preached (Paul writes: 'Of the Jews five times received I forty stripes save one. Thrice was I beaten with rods, once was I stoned', 2 Corinthians 11:24–25). Despite this, the Christian establishment of those early years, based in Jerusalem under the leadership of Jesus' brother James, still saw the teaching of Jesus as aimed at a Jewish audience and fully consistent with the Torah – which meant in turn that they were not sympathetic to efforts to bring in Gentile converts. And in the wider world of Jewry, the level of dispute between Jews and the Roman Empire was steadily increasing.

The key issues that all four Gospel writers had to deal with were the failure of the mission to Jews; the increasing popularity of Christianity among Gentiles; and the delay of the Second Coming. How does Mark tackle these?

Mark's answer to the first question is straightforward. The Jews rejected Jesus *because Jesus had already rejected them*. He did not want them to receive the new Gospel. Mark's Jesus is sharply and consistently critical of the Torah (Mark 7:1–23, 11:27–33). This is bad enough. But Mark's Gospel claims that Jesus made his message deliberately obscure 'lest at any time [the Jews] should be converted, and their sins should be forgiven them', 4:12). The 'messianic secret', Jesus' constant concern to tell no one of his true identity, thus falls into place. Jesus is very selective about who he reveals his true identity to. His status as messiah and Son of God is consistently hidden from Jews until the Passion narrative – or until episodes that refer forward to it. When Jesus asks the disciples who they think he is (8:29), in an episode significantly placed right at the heart of the Gospel, the question feeds directly into a prediction of his coming death and resurrection. (Note also that Jesus neither confirms nor denies the rightness of Peter's claim that he is the messiah, and strictly forbids the disciples to spread the news any further.)

The same pattern recurs a few verses later, after the Transfiguration: 'he charged them that they should tell no man what things they had seen, till the Son of man were risen from the dead' (9:9). Apart from Peter, the only representative of the Jews to identify him as Son of God during his ministry is the high priest (14:61) – and that is during the Passion.

And what of Gentiles? In general they are consistently more receptive to Jesus' teaching and mission. After the Jews conspire to murder him, multitudes stream out from pagan cities to hear him (3:1–9); after quarrelling over purity laws with Pharisees, he is well received in the non-Jewish region of Tyre (Chapter 7); after the Jews have condemned him to crucifixion, the Roman centurion in charge recognises him as the Son of God (15:39). Indeed the only point at which he breaks his policy of enjoining secrecy after a cure is in the Gentile country of the Gerasenes, where he encounters a man with 'an unclean spirit' who identifies him as 'Son of the most high God' (5:7): uniquely, Jesus tells this Gentile to 'Go home to thy friends, and tell them how great things the Lord hath done for thee' (5:19).

What is happening here? Mark is obviously setting out to validate a mission to Gentiles. But he is doing more. He is projecting back into the time of Jesus the differing responses – Jewish hostile, Gentile receptive – experienced by the Christian missionaries of his own time.[36]

What about the relationship between the disciples of Jesus in Jerusalem and the preachers of Jesus in the wider world? It is very striking that Mark is not at all complimentary about the disciples. They are always failing to understand, losing their nerve, wrangling among themselves, failing in faith, falling asleep at critical moments. And when it comes to the crucifixion they are presented as utterly craven: the only one who stays with Jesus is Peter, and even he denies him thrice. The only followers who are present at his crucifixion are the women (15:40–41), and it is these women who note where the body is laid, who go with spices to prepare it for burial, and who discover the miracle of his resurrection. Why is this? Why does Mark present the disciples as so weak and fearful? Because he wants to make a contrast. The famous 'unfinished' ending of Mark (16:8) is deliberately unfinished. It will be completed in Mark's own time by the fall of the Temple and the Second Coming. And as Paula Fredriksen puts it, 'where those who had followed Jesus in his lifetime had failed and fled, those of the first and final Christian generation – Mark's generation – stood faithfully: enduring till the End, awaiting salvation, keeping watch for the return in glory of the Son of Man'.[37]

This in turn explains a number of prophecies that Mark places in the mouth of Jesus. The disciples of Mark's time had to endure violence from many sources – not just beatings from synagogue courts, but attacks from pagans and Romans too. Mark makes Jesus predict this (Chapter 13), consoling the disciples of Jesus' time for the troubles endured by the missionaries of Mark's. Jesus suffers and will triumph; if his followers suffer, they will triumph too.

What about the last question that Mark sets out to answer – the time of the Lord's return? Here is Mark's special brilliance. The fate of Jesus is matched to the fate of the Temple. Jesus' crucifixion is apparently a tragedy, but turns as predicted into a triumphant resurrection. The downfall of the Temple – once again an apparent tragedy – signals the Second Coming of Jesus (13:2–8, 14, 29). The clue in the text ('let him that readeth understand', 13:14), cannot be a record of what Jesus said. He was speaking, not writing. The intended audience is not the hearer of Jesus' speech, but the reader of Mark's writing: one of the elect 'whom he hath chosen', and for whom 'he has shortened the days' (13:20). It is Mark's generation, not Jesus', that will see the return of the Son of Man, and will not pass away 'till all these things be done' (13:26 and 30).

The context of the Gospels of Matthew and Luke (85–95 AD) together with Acts (probably 90–100 AD)

The next two Gospels to be written – Matthew and Luke, written somewhere round 85–95 AD – seem to have been created entirely independently of each other. But they build directly on Mark, and tell a recognisably similar story. Their work has three components.

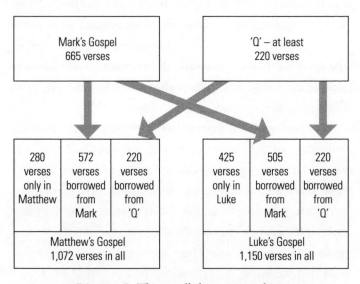

Diagram 7. The so-called two-source theory
(© Paul Beeching, 1997, from Awkward Reverence: Reading the New Testament Today *(Bloomsbury Continuum), used by permission of Bloomsbury Publishing Inc.).*

In part they simply incorporate Mark's own narrative, though with significant amendments. In part they include a text known as 'Q' (from the German *Quelle*, 'source'), a collection of sayings of Jesus that has never itself been found but can confidently be known to exist because both Matthew and Luke incorporate it in virtually identical ways into their stories.[*]

And finally each adds a third component, a very substantial chunk – about a quarter of Matthew and over a third of Luke – of their own devising. It is to Matthew and Luke, not to Mark, that we owe the Nativity stories; the 40-day Temptation in the Wilderness; the Sermon on the Mount; the Lord's Prayer; and the post-Resurrection appearances. So Matthew and Luke are not only redactors – editors of earlier material – but also authors in their own right.

But why were these Gospels needed? Why wouldn't Mark do any longer?

The two new evangelists represent the third generation of the followers of Christ. As such their world was very different from Paul's first-generation world, in which the early followers of Jesus waited expectantly for the return of the leader predicted at the time of the Passion. And it was very different from the world of Mark's second-generation Christians, for whom the fall of Jerusalem had become the signal of the

---

[*] Bishop Papias in the early 2nd century, less than 50 years after Matthew and Luke wrote, tantalisingly refers to an Aramaic collection of Sayings of the Lord made or used by Matthew.

approaching return, and who as a result could once again watch and wait for the Second Coming with lively hope. By the 80s and 90s that hope had faded. It had become clear that those groups that had seemed merely means to an end, places to wait for the coming of the next world, were in fact ends in themselves, communities whose purpose was to live a Christian life in this world and pass on that tradition to their descendants. But how were they to live? What tradition did they themselves inherit, and what would they in turn pass on to their descendants?

Mark, the Gentile writing for Gentiles, could offer no guidance here. Nor could he offer guidance on how to deal with the Jewish element of the faith – its Jewish converts, its Jewish roots, and its need not only to co-exist, but also to define itself against and in competition with the Jewish communities of the Diaspora who still played such a major part in the process of winning new recruits.

What is more, the world in which these third-generation Christians lived had changed radically. Mark's generation had grown up in the shadow of Jerusalem, both as Jewish Temple and as 'mother church' of the Diaspora Christians. Now the Second Temple was gone and with it Jewish Christianity. In its place came a need to honour the founders of Christianity – the Jewish disciples who had been called by Christ himself to follow him.

Finally, the expansion of Christianity had brought with it an expansion of sects and a diversity of teaching. Mark, focused on the imminent Second Coming, had very little to say about this. Now it was time to speak out for the true faith against the false prophets who claimed to speak for it.

We have seen how Mark deals with the three great issues that faced the early Church – the failure of the mission to the Jews, the growing success of the faith among the Gentiles, and the delay of the Second Coming. Matthew and Luke answer these questions in different ways.

Matthew's gospel, in vigorous contrast to Mark's, is the work of a Jew writing for Jews – former Jews who had converted, and practising Jews who had not yet done so. And where Mark's Jesus had deliberately hidden his message, and his true divine nature, from the Jews, Matthew's Jesus aims his message directly at them: 'I am not sent but unto the lost sheep of the house of Israel' (15:24 – this passage is unique to Matthew). This new approach requires Matthew both to rework Mark's text, and to add to it.

Where Mark's Jesus enters the story fully adult, Matthew begins with a birth narrative. It starts 42 generations before birth, providing a genealogy for Jesus that places him squarely in the tradition of Hebrew sacred kingship, starting with Abraham and going via David, the 'once and future king' of Jewish mythology and apocalyptic tradition. Matthew gives Jesus a miraculous birth to a virgin mother, foretold by Isaiah and announced by an angel; he locates his birth in Bethlehem, the birthplace of David; he has Wise Men coming from the

East to kneel and pay homage to the child, showing the submission of Gentiles to Jews; and he follows the birth with a 'descent into Egypt' to escape from Herod, thereby connecting Jesus to another Old Testament hero, in this case also with miraculous origins, Moses.

In Mark, Jesus appears to be rejected even by his own family ('A prophet is not without honour, save in his own country, *and among his own kin*, and in his own house', Mark 3:21, italics added). In Matthew the episode is softened by taking out the passage in italics; Luke (4:24), as we shall see, takes out 'in his own house' as well, thus further weakening any criticism of Jesus' Jewish heritage. Where Mark's twelve apostles are sent out without any limitations (Mark 6:7ff), Matthew's are told firmly to avoid Gentile and Samaritan cities in favour of 'the lost sheep of the house of Israel' (Matthew 10:5–6). And where Mark's Jesus heals the Gerasene demoniac and tells him to proclaim his message to the Gentiles (Mark 5:19), Matthew's version of the story ends with the Gentiles begging him to leave (Matthew 8:34).

Moreover Matthew's Jesus, unlike Mark's, openly reveres the Torah: 'I am come not to destroy, but to fulfil. For verily I say unto you, Till heaven and earth pass, one jot or tittle shall in no wise pass from the law, till all be fulfilled' (Matthew 5:17–18). And Matthew is a massive user of 'proof-texts', passages from the Old Testament used to emphasise Jesus' Jewish roots and to show that his coming fulfils Jewish prophecies from the earliest days: quotations from Micah and Samuel, Jeremiah and Isaiah, are stitched through Matthew's text (see for example 1:22–23; 2:15, 17–18, 23; 4:14–16; 8:17; 12:17–21; 13:35; 21:4–5; 27:9–10), binding the New and the Old Testaments – the Christian and the Hebrew Bibles – into a single unit.

Nor is this all. Matthew places his extracts from Q in five blocks, starting with the Sermon on the Mount, in a way that seems to mirror the five books of the Torah. And the way in which they are presented – 'ye have heard that it was said by them of olden times … but I say unto you' – would be instantly recognisable to a Jew of Matthew's time both as a literary style and as a method of preaching.

What of the disciples? Those passages in which Mark emphasises their dullness, stupidity, and (at the crucifixion) absence, Matthew rewrites. Where Mark's Jesus rebukes the disciples for their lack of understanding (Mark 4:13), Matthew celebrates their good fortune and privileged status (Matthew 13:16–17). Where James and John ask for a special place in the coming Kingdom of God, Matthew attributes the request to their mother (Mark 10:35–45, Matthew 20:20–28; Jewish-mother jokes have a long ancestry …).

When Jesus asks the disciples who they think he is, he criticises Peter harshly both in Matthew and in Mark (Matthew 17:22–23, Mark 8:32–33), but only in Matthew does he also bless him and appoint him head of the new Church (16:17–19). And at the end of the book – a point we will return to – it is the disciples who first receive the new mission, one that includes not only Jews but also Gentiles: 'Go ye therefore, and teach all nations' (Matthew 28:19).

What of diversity of faith? Matthew alone among the four Gospel writers uses the word 'ekklesia', meaning a continuing community of believers united around a single system of belief. He is very insistent on judgement, most famously in the great story of the Last Judgement: 'And before him shall be gathered all nations; and he shall separate them one from another, as a shepherd divideth his sheep from the goats' (25:32). (Curiously the only criterion for salvation here is love, and not even love of God – it is love of one's fellow man!)

However, elsewhere Matthew's pronouncements are much less inclusive. He warns against heresies ('Beware of false prophets', 7:15) and has a parable that appears nowhere else, the Parable of the Tares (13:24–30), with a gloss (13:37–43) explaining how – in another Last Judgement – the Lord will return to assess not only those outside the Church, but those within it. Even Matthew's positive comments on the first disciples after the Resurrection are tempered by a carefully worded hint that even then not all was well ('some doubted', 28:17), suggesting that the different church traditions that so troubled Matthew in his generation had sprung from false transmission of the faith in the earliest days.

Finally there is the difficult question: who is the message of Jesus aimed at? Matthew's Jesus is a Jew preaching to Jews – and yet he closes his Gospel with the magnificent injunction to take the good news to all nations. How does Matthew achieve this transformation? How can Jesus both be sent to the Jews, and sent to the Gentiles? And how can Matthew come, in a book aimed at a Jewish audience, to be the most savage of the evangelists in his condemnation of the Jews' part in Jesus' death?

Matthew's answer is to place Jesus in a long tradition of Jewish prophets – but to explain that *the Jews always reject their prophets*. When Jesus comes to Jerusalem before the Passion, a huge shift takes place in the way he speaks about the Jews. Chapters 21–23 are full of stories about the failure of the Jews to accept the warnings their prophets bring them: the cursing of the fig tree (21:19), the two tales of the vineyard (21:28 and 33), the tale of the wedding banquet (22:2–14), the judgement that 'the kingdom of God shall be taken from you [i.e. the Jews], and given to a nation bringing forth the fruits thereof [i.e. the Gentiles]' (21:43). The rejection of the prophets is itemised in Chapter 23: 'O Jerusalem, Jerusalem, thou that killest the prophets, and stonest them which are sent unto thee' (23:37). And it is reinforced a few verses earlier with a comment strictly from the experience of Christian missionaries of the 90s rather than Jesus' world of the 30s: 'Wherefore, behold, I send unto you prophets, and wise men, and scribes ... and some of them shall ye scourge in your synagogues, and persecute them from city to city' (23:34).

So Matthew draws a distinction between 'good Jews' (the prophets, the holy family, the disciples, Jesus himself) and 'bad Jews' – scribes, Pharisees, and the mob who reject Jesus at the Passion. Mark had explained parables as a way of deliberately hiding the truth from outsiders '*lest* at any time they should be converted, and their sins should be forgiven them' (Mark 4:12, emphasis added), putting the responsibility with

God. Matthew, in a careful rewording, explains that the fault lies with the hearers themselves: 'And in them is fulfilled the prophecy of Esaias [Isaiah], which saith, By hearing ye shall hear, and shall not understand: and seeing ye shall see, and shall not perceive' (Matthew 13:14). In Matthew's account, the Jews were offered salvation, but rejected it. As they always did, they have brought destruction on themselves.

By the end of Matthew's Gospel, the Jews have comprehensively thrown away the chance of salvation for which their whole history was preparing them, offered to them by a Jewish saviour foretold throughout Jewish scripture. Matthew highlights the innocence of Pilate – warned by his wife in a dream, compelled by the Jewish mob, and finally washing his hands of the blood – and the guilt – of the Jews: 'His blood be on us, and on our children' (Matthew 27:25). And the way is clear for Jesus to send his followers out 'to teach all nations' (Matthew 28:18–19).

We have seen how Mark and Matthew dealt with the great issues that faced the early Church. What is Luke's approach?

Before we answer this, there are some points we need to clarify. The first is that Luke actually wrote not one, but two of the books of the New Testament – not only Luke's Gospel, but also the Acts of the Apostles. Although Luke's Gospel is likely to be contemporary with Matthew (85–95 AD), the Acts may be as late as 100 or even later. We don't know, and it isn't critical that we should. Most scholars now refer to Luke–Acts as a single entity; for our purposes here I will take them one after the other to follow the careful development of Luke's arguments over the two books.

'Careful' is a good word for Luke. Here is the opening of his Gospel:

> 'Forasmuch as many have taken in hand to set forth in order a declaration of those things which are most surely believed among us, Even as they delivered them unto us, which from the beginning were eyewitnesses, and ministers of the word; It seemed good to me also, having had perfect understanding of all things from the very first, to write unto thee in order, most excellent Theophilus, That thou mightest know the certainty of those things, wherein thou hast been instructed.'
> (Luke 1:1–4)

This prologue – modelled on the standard introduction to Greek histories of the time – defines his values: measured, thorough, judicious, recognising the great distance that separates him from the events he is writing about, but confident that truth can be sifted from rumour. We think of the 2010 Saville Inquiry into the events of Bloody Sunday: twelve years in the making and 38 years after the event itself, but authoritative enough, when it finally appeared, to cause a Prime Minister to apologise to Parliament. Theophilus, incidentally, may be a real person or a symbol (it means 'lover of God' in

Greek), but if it is a real person, the designation 'most excellent' indicates that it is someone of high status (perhaps like the person who commissioned the Saville Inquiry).

Luke's character shines through both books. His language is both beautiful and flexible, varying in character from the pure Greek of this prologue, through the more archaic Septuagint Greek of his Nativity story (probably following the style of its unknown source), and on to the unpolished *koine* Greek of Acts. His view of history is always a kind and inclusive one, supporting the underdog, bridging over conflicts, looking to overcome contradictions, and trying to be fair to both sides of every argument. In his Gospel, this comes through most clearly in the way it is structured, and before we answer the three questions above, we must briefly explain how his Gospel is put together.

As we have seen, Matthew and Luke both build on Mark, and both include material from Q, the mysterious and missing sayings of Jesus. But both evangelists also add much material of their own. Matthew's own contribution comes to fractionally over a quarter of the Gospel that bears his name: 280 of his 1,072 verses are neither Q nor Mark. Luke's Gospel is of very similar length (1,150 verses); but 425 of these, or over a third, are from Luke himself. These contributions are very revealing. Where would we be without the parable of the Good Samaritan? Or the Return of the Prodigal Son? How can we forget Dives and Lazarus, or Mary and Martha? And what about the story of the Pharisee and the tax collector?

'Two men went up into the temple to pray: the one a Pharisee, and the other a publican [tax collector]. The Pharisee stood and prayed thus with himself, God, I thank thee, that I am not as other men are, extortioners, unjust, adulterers, or even as this publican. I fast twice in the week, I give tithes of all that I possess. And the publican, standing afar off, would not lift up so much as his eyes unto heaven, but smote upon his breast, saying, God be merciful to me a sinner. I tell you, this man went down to his house justified rather than the other.' (Luke 18:10–14)

The most striking aspect of Luke's own contributions to the Gospel story is his concern for women. This starts with the infancy narrative – of which more below – and goes on throughout the book: the raising of the widow's son at Nain (7:11–17), the woman who bathes Jesus' feet with tears (7:36–50), the women who accompany and help to fund Jesus and the disciples (8:2–3), the healing of a crippled woman on the Sabbath (13:11–13), the lamentation for the daughters of Jerusalem (23:28–31). All the Synoptics credit the women with finding the empty tomb; but only Luke points out their forethought in getting the spices they needed for the burial before the shops shut (24:1)!

So – how does this gentle, courteous, urbane Greek-speaker deal with the three burning questions?

In his Gospel, Luke's position is very different from that of his Synoptic colleagues. Luke sees Jesus as eagerly awaited by the people of Israel, who widely welcomed him and were largely willing to accept the new faith. *Consequently he denies that the mission to Jews has failed.*

Luke's Saviour is universal and inclusive. By creating a genealogy that goes back, not as in Matthew to Abraham, the founder of the Hebrews, but to Adam, the founder of humanity, he includes all the branches of the human race (Luke 3:38). By sending the Angel Gabriel to Mary, and by giving her the great hymn we know as the Magnificat, he emphasises the importance of women (Chapter 1). By placing the birth of Jesus in a stable and announcing him first to shepherds, he includes all classes of society (2:7–16). And Jesus' Jewish identity is proudly affirmed by his birth in Bethlehem, by his circumcision, by his presentation at the Temple, and by Simeon and Anna, devout Jews, who see the baby and recognise him as 'the Lord's Christ … A light to lighten the Gentiles, and the glory of thy people Israel' (2: 26, 32). (Anna even speaks of 'redemption in Jerusalem', 2:38.)

Luke is at pains to rehabilitate the (Jewish) disciples that Mark had so severely criticised. Rewriting the account he inherited from Mark, he praises them as 'they which have continued with me in my temptations'; he promises that they will 'sit on thrones judging the twelve tribes of Israel'; and when Jesus finds them sleeping in the garden of Gethsemane the night before his crucifixion, Luke explains that it is 'for sorrow' (22:28, 30, and 45). Where Mark and Matthew have two bandits crucified alongside Jesus who (like the passers-by) taunt and revile him, Luke has one of the bandits ask for, and receive, mercy: 'To day [*sic*] shalt thou be with me in paradise'

(23:43). Where Matthew's Jesus was in the outsider tradition of the prophets, Luke's Jesus is a fully paid up, mainstream Jew, supported by the whole sweep of Jewish history and the full weight of the Torah (24:25–27, 44–47).

As Paula Fredriksen puts it, 'Luke's Jesus is a traditionally pious Jew (e.g. 4:16), who even as a child engaged Jewish teachers in dialogue and awed them with his understanding (2:46)'.[38] He even has supporters among the Pharisees: although annoyed by his violations of the Sabbath (6:11, 13:10–17, 14:1–6), they try to persuade him to flee when he is endangered by Herod Antipas (13:31–33). Who does oppose and harass him? The chief priests and scribes (19:47 and 20:19–26; note that Luke omits any mention of the Pharisees in these episodes). The Roman centurion whose slave Jesus heals appears also in Mark, but Luke characteristically adapts Mark to tell us that the Gentile centurion is also aligned with the Jews: 'For he loveth our nation, and he hath built us a synagogue' (Luke 7:5).

Luke's treatment of the Temple is particularly revealing. The Cleansing of the Temple that is so important in Mark and Matthew is allocated only two verses in Luke (19:45–46), and he omits Mark's and Matthew's prophecies of the destruction of the Temple at Jesus' trial and crucifixion. What is more, after the crucifixion the apostles honour the Sabbath, resting 'according to the commandment' (23:56); the good news of Jesus is to be proclaimed to all nations, but 'beginning at Jerusalem' (24:47); and the Gospel ends with the apostles continually praising God – where else? – 'in the temple' (24:53).

Mark has the Jews calling for the death of Jesus: Matthew even has them explicitly accepting responsibility for that death. How does Luke treat this? He clearly cannot avoid implicating the Jews in the crucifixion because like his fellow Synoptics, he has to find a way to exculpate the Romans. Accordingly he has Jesus judged by the Sanhedrin and brought by them before Pilate. But his treatment of the events is very different from both Mark and Matthew. Around this rejection by the people, he wraps their adulation in the run-up to the Passion (Luke 19:48, 20:26, 21:38) and their grief and sorrow on the very day of the crucifixion: by contrast with the taunting abuse of Mark and Matthew's watchers, Luke's Jesus is followed by grieving women; gives up his life with the tranquil, 'Father, into thy hands I commend my spirit' (23:46) rather than Mark's anguished 'My God, my God, why hast thou forsaken me?' (Mark 15:34); and is mourned by repentant crowds (Luke 23:27 and 48). Only in Luke do we find the famous saying from the cross, 'Father, forgive them; for they know not what they do' (23:34).

So Luke in his Gospel answers the first two questions very similarly: the mission has succeeded, or at least had a considerable impact, both with Jews and with non-Jews. What of the third question, the delay in the Second Coming?

It seems that Luke could not avoid citing some of the familiar warning passages, most notably in Chapter 21, which echoes fairly closely Mark 13 and Matthew 24. In particular, rather puzzlingly, he exactly follows both Mark and Matthew in the famous verse in which Jesus promises that he will return in the lifetime of his hearers ('Verily I say unto you, This gen-eration shall not pass away, till all be fulfilled' – Luke 21:32; compare Mark 13:30 and Matthew 24:34 for an identical message). And he also suggests that the fall of Jerusalem – a matter of history by the time Luke wrote – will be a sign of the Second Coming (Luke 21:20–28). This is strange for two reasons: first, and obviously, because by the time of Matthew and Luke it clearly had not happened; and second, because it does not correspond to the emphasis elsewhere in Luke, and in Acts, on the idea that what matters is not the Second Coming, but the first – Jesus' message and his resurrection – and its consequences for the community of believers. Perhaps he simply had to put in this material because it was so well known. We shall never know!

But for the most part Luke avoids the whole idea of a delay in the Second Coming. First, he unobtrusively lengthens the timescale. Mark promises that the Lord 'hath shortened the days [until the Second Coming]' (Mark 13:20). Matthew, in a verse that otherwise follows Mark almost word for word, subtly varies the timing, promising only that those days 'shall be shortened' (Matthew 24:22). Luke omits the phrase entirely. Where Mark's Jesus tells the high priest that he 'shall see the Son of Man sitting on the right hand of power, and coming in the clouds of heaven' (Mark 14:62), Luke's Jesus promises only that the Son of Man 'shall sit on the right hand of the power of God' (Luke 22:69). But most importantly, he gets over the idea of a delay by asserting that the Kingdom *has arrived already*. Where Mark's 'Kingdom' will come only when Jesus returns in power, Luke's 'Kingdom of God' is present with the earthly Jesus and the faith of his followers: 'The kingdom of God cometh not with observation ... for behold, the kingdom of God is within you' (Luke 17:20–21; see also 8:1, 9:2, 10:9).

This leaves us with only one question to resolve – but it is a sticky one. The Luke of the Gospel may assert that the Jews have been receptive to the message of Jesus; but the Luke of Acts knows that by the time at which he wrote, they had by and large rejected it. If the Gospel does not explain the failure of the mission to the Jews, how does Acts explain it?

Acts has been well described as having two parts: the Acts of Peter (the first half), and the Acts of Paul. The initial mission from the risen Jesus commands the apostles to bear witness 'in Jerusalem, and in all Judea, and in Samaria, and unto the uttermost part of the earth' (Acts 1:8). Very soon this becomes a reality with the experience of speaking in tongues at the feast of Pentecost: the 120 believers in Jerusalem find themselves speaking diverse languages* to 'Jews, devout men, out of every nation under heaven' (2:5, 9–11), and Peter makes a splendid speech acknowledging the part played by the Jews in the death of Jesus, but explaining that this death was 'by the determinate counsel and foreknowledge of God' (2:23) and offering to his Jewish audience the opportunity to repent and be baptised (2:38). (Characteristically, Luke shows them as 'pricked in their heart' – Acts 2:37.) So successful is this appeal

---

* This is Luke's misunderstanding of the phrase 'speaking in tongues'.

that 3,000 new recruits add themselves to the faith (2:41). This process is repeated soon afterwards, again with the emphasis that the Jews and their rulers acted in ignorance (3:17), with even greater success in the form of a further 5,000 souls (4:4).

The first Jewish resistance comes from the high priest and the Sadducees, 'filled with indignation' (5:17–18) and probably less than enthusiastic about the constant reminders of their part in Jesus' death. But despite prison and flogging the apostles continue to teach and preach 'daily in the temple' (5:42), to the point where 'a great company of the priests were obedient to the faith' (6:7).

What seems to be a decisive break occurs when Stephen reproaches the high priest and members of the Temple Council for their habit of killing prophets. Not surprisingly, the council members are enraged at this and stone Stephen to death (with the assistance of Saul, soon to be Paul). This leads to a severe persecution in Jerusalem, but the faith continues to spread: the surviving apostles just move on to Judea and Samaria and thence to Caesarea (Acts 8), Lydda, and Joppa (modern Jaffa). By Chapter 9 the word has got out as far as Phoenicia, Cyprus and Antioch (11:19), and the believers from these Diaspora cities are even persuaded to get together a collection for famine relief back home in Judea (11:27–30).

From Acts 13 the focus shifts from Peter (increasingly concerned with Israel) to Paul: 'the Holy Ghost said, Separate me Barnabas and Saul for the work whereunto I have called them' (13:2). And this is where the real trouble starts. In each new Gentile city they visit, Paul and Barnabas do the obvious thing:

they go to the synagogue to preach. Why? For a variety of reasons. First, because as practising Jews it is their natural home, the obvious place to 'check in'. Second, because they want to spread the word to the Jewish congregation who worship there. But there is a third reason that is more double-edged. Synagogues, as we have seen, attracted 'God-fearers', pious Gentiles drawn to the Jewish faith and practice by its ethical teaching, its historical depth, its developed religious practice, and its support of its own poor and needy. So how is it going to be if a different branch of Judaism – the Christian branch – suddenly breezes into the synagogue and starts trying to win over not only the Jews, but also the God-fearers? A branch that blames the Jews (not the God-fearers) for killing its Saviour, and insists on Jewish repentance as a precondition for conversion?

There was yet another reason for Diaspora Jews to be very wary of the Christian missionaries. The message of the early Christians, as we have seen, focused powerfully on the approaching 'end days' – the Second Coming of Jesus. The natural consequence of this was to abandon the ordinary practices of life in order to dedicate oneself to preparation for the life to come. We know from various of Paul's letters (notably 2 Thessalonians 3) that this was an unintended consequence of early Christian preaching. But such behaviour was not just a nuisance. It could also be a danger. Anti-Jewish riots were not unknown: Tiberius expelled the Jews from Rome in 18 AD and Claudius did likewise around 49 (as Luke mentions in Acts 18:2); and there had been a pogrom in Alexandria in 38. Stirring up discontent would be seen by the elders of the synagogue as highly provocative to the local community. (We remember the decision of the high priest to hand over Jesus to prevent riots at the Passover in Jerusalem.) In such circumstances, God-fearers were not just potential converts; equally importantly, they were friends, allies, and supporters in a world in which the Jewish community were immigrants – 'strangers in a strange land' – and in a small and defenceless minority.

So the early missionaries were in something of a bind. The synagogue was the obvious place for them to go, and the most fertile ground for them to plough; and yet it was also where they represented the greatest threat. And in Luke's account, this is indeed where the relationship between the Jews and the early Christians turns sour. Time after time – Antioch, Iconium, Lystra, Thessalonica, Beroea, Corinth, Achaia – Paul and his fellow missionaries repeat the same pattern: a warm welcome and an invitation to speak when they call in at the local synagogue, a lively response to their talk from Jews and non-Jews alike, and then, a week later, a bitter resistance from the local (or neighbouring) synagogue authorities.

The pattern of strife with the Temple authorities is repeated, for different reasons, when Paul returns to Jerusalem (Acts 21:27–32), but finally Paul sets sail for Rome, and there he finds the same mixed reception (28:24). And only then does Acts finally and definitively answer the question posed in Luke's Gospel: how do we account for the non-success of the mission to Jews?

'Well spake the Holy Ghost by Esaias the prophet unto our fathers, Saying, Go unto this people, and say, Hearing ye shall hear, and shall not understand; and seeing ye shall see, and not perceive ... Be it known therefore unto you, that the salvation of God is sent unto the Gentiles, and that they will hear it.' (Acts 28:25–28)

The villains of the piece are the Jews of the Diaspora. The crime of killing Jesus could be and had been forgiven; the crime of turning away his message, could not.

The Gospel according to John (probably two stages, c. 70 AD and c. 95 AD)

Who is this who comes in splendour, coming from the
  blazing East?
This is he we had not thought of, this is he the airy Christ
                 (Stevie Smith, 'The Airy Christ')*

The last of the four Gospels is 'According to John' (though there is no certainty as to who this John was). What kind of work is it? Well, as the quotation above implies, the reader should prepare for a shock. Paula Fredriksen points out that 'John's Jesus is not the wandering charismatic Galilean who appears [in Matthew, Mark, and Luke], but an enigmatic

---

* To my surprise, I find that Stevie Smith's poem was actually composed about Mark's Jesus, but it fits John's so well that I have borrowed it for that purpose.

visitor from the cosmos above'.[39] This Jesus does not talk in the rough, agricultural language of his farming background. He speaks a language of light and darkness, of above and below, of Water and Spirit, of the Bread of Life, of the Vine and the Branches: he uses the Temple as a metaphor for his body, and the cross as a metaphor for being lifted up to heaven, and constantly speaks in riddles. The witty, earthy, cheeky boy of Mark's Gospel could not be further away: this is an aloof, solitary, passionate dreamer from another planet, who, like the hero of Isherwood's 1962 novel, is only 'down here on a visit'.

Indeed John's Gospel is so different that right up until the 4th century the Church hesitated as to whether to include it in the canon: some Church fathers, known as the *alogoi* ('those who reject John's *logos* theology'), refused to accept it at all.

How did John's Gospel come into being? For many years it was thought to be very late indeed – perhaps as late as 150–200 AD – because of the very distinctive 'Gnostic' quality of its thought (see below). But we now know that Gnosticism was active much earlier; material from John's Gospel has been found dating to about 130, and most current scholars think it was composed in two stages, the earlier around 70 AD, the later around 95.[40]

One consequence of this two-stage and perhaps two-author theory is that it helps to explain some of the extra-ordinary muddles in the text. Chapters 5 and 6 are out of order: in Chapter 5 Jesus leaves Galilee, and in Chapter 6 he is back in Galilee. This difficulty is easily fixed by reversing the order of the two chapters. But in 7:21 Jesus says he has performed only one miracle: the text says he has performed at least four. In the very next verse Jesus states that Moses ordered circumcision, whereupon the editor rather brusquely corrects him (7:22). In 12:36 Jesus 'departed and did hide himself from them', but by 12:44 without any warning he is back preaching again. In 13:36 Peter asks him where he is going: in 16:5 Jesus complains that no one asks him where he is going ... and so on.

Overall, John leaves out a great number of what we have come to consider essential elements of the Christian narrative. The broad outlines of the story are recognisable: John's Jesus meets the Baptist, preaches, performs miracles, goes to Jerusalem, is crucified, and rises again. But the similarity hides profound differences. John leaves out many of the elements that emphasise the physical nature of Jesus: no birth story, no actual Baptism, no Temptation, no Sermon on the Mount, no parables, no Eucharist at the Last Supper. Conversely he puts a lot in, notably miracles such as the Raising of Lazarus and stories such as Doubting Thomas, and – perhaps most famously – the Woman Caught in Adultery (John 8:1–11). The timescale for the preaching of Jesus is different, with three years allowed for it, and multiple visits to Jerusalem, rather than the single packed year of the Synoptics. And even more than Luke, John writes in a highly formal style using a range of complex structures drawn from Greek rhetoric.

We know the historical context of this period because it is the same as Luke, and to some extent as Matthew: the rise of rabbinical Judaism, the 'Diaspora Wars' that arose as an increasingly Gentile faith tried to win converts through the network of Jewish synagogues, and a growing bitterness between different branches of the new faith. To this we can add an increasing climate of Gnosticism, an attitude to the world with deep roots in Persian mysticism but which flourished in Hellenist, and in parts of Jewish, mysticism in the early centuries of the Christian era. In Gnosticism, flesh and the world of matter are inherently fallen and evil. Salvation is through Spirit: it comes to those 'Which were born, not of blood, nor of the will of the flesh, nor of the will of man, but of God' (John 1:13). John wrote in the Gnostic tradition. Against this context, how does John answer the three questions that so troubled the early Church: the lack of success among the Jews, the relative success among the Gentiles, and the delay of the Second Coming?

Unlike Luke, John agrees that the Jews have rejected Jesus. Writing rather later than Mark, he has more evidence to go on: by the 80s there is evidence that Jewish Christians, and perhaps Gentile Christians too, were not welcome in synagogues, and John (anachronistically) makes Jesus refer to this in 9:22 and 16:2. His explanation for this is the same as Mark's, quoting Isaiah 6:10 to show that in fact Israel did not reject the mission: it was never really offered to them. The Lord has 'blinded their eyes, and hardened their heart' (John 12:40; see also 5:44–47, 8:19 and 47, and 10:26–27). His references to the Jews are off-hand, distant, dismissive: 'the Jews' Passover was at hand', 2:13, 'as the manner of the Jews is to bury', 19:40. With a final flourish, John makes the Chief Priests (of all people) say that 'We have no king but Caesar' (19:15)! And like Mark, John is not concerned about this because his Jesus comes not to the many, but to the few: 'He came unto his own, and his own received him not. But as many as received him ... to them gave he power to become the sons of God' (John 1:11–12; see also 6:44–51, 8:19, and passim).

So John's Jesus includes Samaritans (Chapter 4) and Gentiles in his preaching: 'Other sheep I have, which are not of this fold: them also I must bring, and they shall hear my voice' (10:16). But he knows that the flock will not be a big one.

What of the delay of the Second Coming? Here we come to the nub of the question. *In John's Gospel, Jesus is not of this world – and nor is his kingdom* (18:36; see also 5:24, 15:19, 16:33). John's Gnostic roots enable him to sidestep the requirement for a crusading messiah to return in glory and transform the world. John has 'a high Christology' – he is absolutely emphatic that Jesus is the Son of God, rather than just another prophet, and that at his death Jesus will return to his place at the right hand of God. But John has no expectation that Jesus will return to earth to fight the messianic fight and liberate Judea. His kingdom is not of this world. So when will he come again? There is no need to come again. There has been no delay. *His kingdom has already arrived.* 'Be of good cheer: I have overcome the world' (16:33). Where Mark's Jesus wrestles with fear, pain, and despair at his crucifixion, John's progresses serenely to the cross as to a coronation, and dies with tranquillity: 'It is finished' (19:30). The horizontal axis of Mark – from present awaiting, to future return – has in a sense gone vertical: the only movement is a timeless one, from below to above.

This solves three major problems for the new faith. First, it avoids the difficult question – hard enough for believing Christians, and exceptionally difficult for Christian missionaries trying to clarify the faith to non-believers – of when to expect the return of the Lord. Second, it differentiates the new faith from Judean messianic expectations – and in doing so, defines another way in which Christianity has moved on from its Jewish roots. And finally, perhaps most importantly, it explains to any potential Roman critics that Christians are not dissidents, revolutionaries, millenarians, terrorists. 'My kingdom is not of this world ...'.

So John has performed a major feat: one of enormous importance to the current and future fortunes of Christianity. He has made Jesus safe. Salvation has moved from this world to another one; from outer action to inner state; from Marx to Maharishi.

Is this enough about John? Not quite. Curiously, John's Gospel – so remote, so other-worldly, so unconcerned with practical details – seems actually more reliable than the Synoptics in the few concrete details that it does give. Where the Synoptics allow Jesus only a year's ministry and a single visit to Jerusalem, John allows him three or four, and tells us that during the first year Jesus was almost arrested (7:32), as he was on his final visit (11:57). The Cleansing of the Temple occurs much earlier (John 2:13–16) and cannot therefore be the trigger for the arrest. The way Jesus is treated by the Temple authorities on his sequence of Passover visits to Jerusalem fits well with the theory advanced by Elias Bickerman,[41] according to which Jesus was outlawed by the Roman authorities, with a price on his head, on the first visit and therefore remained in hiding – or in such a public place that the crowds would protect him – on his subsequent Passover visits. When Judas betrays him, he knows the place that Jesus regularly hides (John 18:2); the squad sent to arrest him consists of both Jewish police and Roman soldiers, as befits an outlaw. As a known outlaw he is bound at once (18:12); and for the same reason, no trial before the Sanhedrin is required. Jesus has form and can be passed straight to the governor for sentence.

There are several other places in which John's account is persuasive. As we have seen, the timing of the Last Supper is a problem in the accounts of the Synoptics: John solves the difficulty, placing it a day earlier, on the Thursday, the night before the Passover Festival (13:1). And John's report of the Resurrection (20:1–18) is extraordinarily spare and concrete when set against the rather overwrought accounts in Matthew, Mark, and Luke. Curiously, John the story-teller speaks very differently from John the Gnostic theologian, and we cannot but be reminded of the moments when the writer, speaking as 'the disciple whom Jesus loved', claims to have personally witnessed the events he writes of (13:23–26, 19:35, 21:7, 21:24) – a claim not made in similar fashion by any of the Synoptics.

And there is still more to say about John. Much of his Gnosticism has not worn well: the teaching is often repetitive and wearisome and one is not surprised to hear that at one point 'many of his disciples went back, and walked no more with him' (6:66). But for all its oddities, John's Gospel still gives us some of the most memorable, magnificent, and consoling passages of the whole Bible. The mysterious, awe-inspiring opening of the Gospel, with its deliberate echoes of Genesis ('In the beginning was the Word'); the softness and embracing warmth of his care for his disciples ('For God so loved the world, that he gave his only begotten Son, that whosoever believeth in him should not perish, but have everlasting life … I am the good shepherd: the good shepherd giveth his life for his sheep … In the world ye shall have tribulation: but be of good cheer; I have overcome the world', 3:16, 10:11–12, 16:33); the inclusive power of 'I came not to judge the world, but to save the world' (12:47); and the breathtaking, 'Greater love hath no man than this, that a man lay down his life for his friends'* (15:13). We remember that John alone has the wonderful verse, 'Jesus wept' (11:35).

Perhaps the best place to leave John is where we began, with Stevie Smith:

---

* 'Friend', alas, is not what it seems: the word here and in 19:12 is used in the sense of 'client' or 'subordinate partner', rather than the equal relationship we always assume. See *New Oxford Annotated Bible,* p. 1907. The passage is a striking example of a translation that is better than the original …

... he does not wish that men should love him more than
  anything
Because he died: he only wishes they would hear him sing
                                (Stevie Smith, 'The Airy Christ')

How was the New Testament put together?

Before turning to Jesus himself as he is presented in the Bible,
we need to round off this part of our account by briefly exam-
ining how we come to have the canon of 27 books that form
the New Testament as we have it now. ('Canon', from the
Greek word for yardstick, was used by literary critics in the
ancient world to define the body of literary texts they thought
worthy of study.)

As we have seen, the scattered 'house churches' of the
1st century AD, each with its own doctrine and practice, rapidly felt the need for a consistent body of teaching. By about
150 AD a single body of texts, including the four Gospels, was
accepted as 'canonical' throughout the expanding Christian
world. (The differences between the four Gospels were well
known even then, and a document that edited and spliced
them into one, the *Diatessaron*, was written by Tatian around
160 AD and widely used.) We have seen that the Torah, the
powerhouse of the Old Testament, was edited and recast by
one man, the scribe Ezra. Is there a similar process at work
with the New Testament?

From one point of view, the answer is a definite no. The
four Gospels each have a different setting and purpose: the
early letters of Paul are indeed largely or completely the work

of Paul, an entirely independent mind, and the later letters, together with the Revelation of St John, seem to be equally individual and independent. If these documents do cohere and converge, it is not – as in the Old Testament – because someone smoothed them into a harmony.

However, there is another way in which harmony can be created, and that is by selection. Does the New Testament represent all the writings of the early Christians?

The New Testament as we have it represents works composed before (say) 120 AD – and for the most part before 100 AD. Do we know of any accounts of Jesus from this time that are not included? There is only one, the so-called 'Gospel of Thomas', a collection of sayings attributed to Jesus that was (re)discovered in the Nag Hammadi finds in Egypt in 1945. The date of original composition is uncertain, and the contents, though in a few cases very recognisable, are often extremely strange. Certainly it does not seem a great loss to the New Testament.

So the early Church used all, or almost all, the material they had to hand in order to put together a canon. How was it used? Interestingly, the first canon that we know of was proposed around 140 AD by Marcion, who declared that Christianity was discontinuous with Judaism and that the Christian God of universal benevolence was entirely different from the vengeful tribal God of the Old Testament. (This may strike some readers as rather familiar …) Accordingly, and crucially, his canon did not contain any works from the Old Testament.

The response was immediate and decisive. Marcion's canon was rejected and Marcion himself excommunicated. By 200 AD there was agreement on the backbone of the present Bible – not just four Gospels and ten Epistles, but also the whole of the Hebrew Bible or Old Testament. Some of the Epistles remained in dispute, but the final New Testament canon as we have it now was definitely established by 367 AD.

What of the post-100 AD writings that did not make it into the canon? There are a lot of them! It seems that there was a tremendous appetite for materials to fill the gaps in the four Gospels. Thus we have apocryphal stories of the infancy of Jesus: of his descent to Hades, including the raising of Adam, the patriarchs, and the prophets; of his resurrection; of the (further) acts of the apostles; of the further career of Pilate; and apocryphal letters, apocalypses, and revelations. What can we say about these voluminous writings from the period 100–300 AD?

First, that they reflect the concerns (and curiosities) of the early Christians – their passionate appetite for the 'back story' behind the Gospel. These are the *Hello* magazine, the Facebook, the blogs and tweets, of their time. They are personal, magical, emotional, sensational. Good characters are caught up into heaven, wicked characters are immersed to their knees (very wicked ones to their necks) in boiling lava, pus, or faeces, and the star performers of the Gospels and Acts get a sequel, or a prequel, to ensure that every possible information gap is filled. Some of these stories are exceedingly odd. In the 'Infancy Gospel of Thomas' (IGT), for example, the child Jesus strikes down two teachers who have offended him (IGT 14, 15:7), and kills a number of fellow pupils who irritate him (IGT 3:2). Pontius Pilate is presented in such a positive light in 'Paradosis Pilati' that the Coptic and Ethiopian churches have made him a saint. In the 'Acts of Paul', a lion is baptised; in the 'Acts of Peter', Peter revives a dead fish; and in the apocryphal 'Acts of John', the hero rebukes bedbugs who have interrupted his sleep, and one of the characters attempts to rape a corpse.

Secondly, they remind us of the struggle in the New Testament – and the Hebrew Bible – between realism and romance. Looking at the Acts of the Apostles after reading the apocryphal version of the same stories, we recognise in the canonical text so many examples of the same urge to romantic exaggeration: the way that Peter's shadow and Paul's handkerchiefs cause miraculous cures (Acts 5:12–16, 19:11–12), the magical disappearance of Philip after baptising the eunuch (Acts 8:39), the striking dead of Ananias and Sapphira (Acts 5:1–11), the thrilling sea stories (Acts 27) – all these remind us that sacred myth and secular romance, scripture and folktale, obey very similar conventions.[42]

The third point to make in relation to these post-New Testament writings is a simple one. They are of interest to the scholar, and to the author of *The Da Vinci Code*. They need not detain the rest of us!

7. Who did Jesus think he was?

> 'On the eve of Passover they hanged Yeshu [Jesus] and the
> herald went before him for forty days saying, "Yeshu is
> going forth to be stoned in that he hath practised sorcery
> and beguiled and led astray Israel. Let everyone knowing
> aught in his defence come and plead for him". But they
> found naught in his defence and hanged him on the eve
> of Passover.'
>
> (Babylonian Talmud, 5th–6th century AD)*

No study of the New Testament can avoid the central question
– who was Jesus? In this final section I want to ask three questions. In each case I shall look for answers, not in the sphere
of faith, but in the domain of scholarship: not in the Bible as
sacred text, but in the Bible as historical record.

The first question is, who did Jesus' hearers think he was?
What categories did they have to understand and interpret
him and his message?

Secondly – a question that has much exercised recent New
Testament scholars – why was Jesus crucified, yet his followers
were not?

And finally, and most ambitiously – who did Jesus think
he was?

---

* I am grateful to John Clarke, former Dean of Wells Cathedral,
for this reference.

The Christ of faith and the Jesus of history

Let us begin by defining our terms. For over a century, scholars have distinguished between the Christ of faith (the divine figure worshipped by believers) and the Jesus of history, the man studied by historians. The Christ of faith looks forward to our times and beyond. The Jesus of history looks at his own times, and in a sense we see only his back: his gaze is turned to the men and women of his own time, whose language he had to speak, and whose beliefs he had to understand, in order to convey his message.

This book is not intended to examine the Christ of faith: it can speak only of the Jesus of history. The writers of the New Testament – most strikingly in the case of Paul, but very evidently in all the Gospel writers – had no interest in the historical Jesus. As Paul Beeching puts it, their eye was firmly on 'the truth of meaning' rather than 'the truth of reference' and 'their gospels were … exercises in theology'.[43] It might therefore seem that all hope of historical accuracy is lost; but that would be a mistake.

First, we know that some elements of the New Testament (as with the Old) are there because they are inconvenient truths that the Gospel writers couldn't set aside. The towering presence of John the Baptist, forerunner and baptiser of Jesus and leader (both during and after his life) of a rival cult; the insistence that the message was only for Jews; the urgent predictions of the imminent Second Coming; even the crucifixion itself – these are historical icebergs, too big to break through, that the narrative has to navigate around. Second, these texts are of their time – within a century of the events they are writing about – and can tell us much of the circumstances, the assumptions, and the beliefs, of Jesus' own period. And finally, if they record the beliefs and expectations of a rural Galilean audience, then inevitably they record, at least in part, the beliefs and expectations of their rural Galilean hero.

So let us look at the events of Jesus' life from a strictly historical viewpoint, trying to sift the Jesus of history from the Christ of faith.

The Christ of faith	The Jesus of history
Ancestry, birth, descent into Egypt	
	Baptism by John
	Preaching
	Incident in Temple
	Entry into Jerusalem
	Final meal
	Arrest at Gethsemane
	Appearance before high priest
Trial before Pilate	
Condemnation by Jewish crowd	
	Crucifixion
Burial	
Resurrection	

There is no intention here to suggest that the events of the left-hand side did not happen; only that however visible to the eye of faith, they cannot reliably be inspected through the lens of history.

Miracles

One element missing from the list above is 'miracles'. Miracles are a much misunderstood topic. Non-believers discount them as proof of the falsehood of the Gospel; believers emphasise them as proofs of the holiness of Christ and his closeness to, or indeed identity with, God.

Both are mistaken.

Miracle: 'a surprising or welcome event that is not explicable by natural or scientific laws and is therefore considered to be the work of a divine agency' (*Oxford English Dictionary*). Since the 18th-century Enlightenment we have become conditioned to think of miracles as happening far outside the sphere of normality. But the ancient world did not think in this way. (Nor, if we judge by *Hamlet* and *Macbeth*, did the Elizabethans!) Miracles were a surprise and a source of amazement ('*miraculum*, object of wonder', *OED*). But plenty of people claimed to be able to perform them. Jesus performed miracles, but he was able to pass this skill on to his disciples ('They cast out many demons, and anointed with oil many who were sick and cured them', Mark 6:13 and similarly in Matthew and Luke), and they in turn passed the power on to others in Acts (where, as we have seen, even Paul's shadow and Peter's handkerchief can heal disease). Geza Vermes records the miracles of Honi the Circle Drawer and Hanina ben Dosa.[44]

And if good guys – Moses, Elijah, Elisha – could perform miracles, so could bad guys: Pharaoh's wise men and sorcerers turned their staffs into snakes (Exodus 7:11–12), and Simon Magus amazed the people of Samaria with his magic (Acts 8:9–11). Power was not confined to magicians: Roman emperors, Greek sages (Apollonius of Tyana was said to have raised a girl from the dead), and even English monarchs performed wonders – the King's Evil is the medieval name for a skin disease that the ruler's touch was believed to cure. And power was not confined to the powerful: itinerant wonder-workers, practising magic for a fee, were a regular feature of rural life in Galilee. In short, and however strange to us today, magic and miracle – the one done by 'them', the other by 'us' – are part of the fabric of the ancient world: they are not a proof of special holiness, and certainly not of divinity.

So Jesus' hearers believed that he performed miracles. Who would his hearers have thought he was? What was in the minds of the cheering crowds who strewed palm leaves before him and cried 'Hosanna' ('Save us') as he rode into Jerusalem on a donkey? The answer is of course that they thought he was the messiah – the anointed of the Lord, come to restore Israel to her ancient greatness and to throw off the yoke of Rome. We cannot tell if they expected him to be a peaceful messiah, an Elijah or a Moses, or a warlike messiah in the mould of King David: but the crowds who had followed Theudas and the Egyptian (see page 130), who would soon rally to the defence of Jerusalem, and who would a century later fight in the rebellion of Simon bar Kochba, were animated by the same expectation of divine support and divine power. The people of Jesus' time had no expectation of a crucified messiah and no framework to fit one into: the crucifixion would have proved to them beyond doubt that Jesus was not the messiah.

The Jesus of history: how Jesus saw himself

If the Jewish crowds projected their own expectations onto Jesus, who do modern historians think he believed himself to be? I shall confine myself to the writings of scholars who are also believers and so have no atheist or agnostic axe to grind. After nearly a century in which historians felt the topic was exhausted, there has been a huge resurgence of interest in the quest for the historical Jesus. He is seen as a Cynic philosopher, as a Jewish sage, as a political agitator and rebel with an agenda of social justice, and as a passionate prophet of the approaching End Time.[45] In addition a Jewish perspective has been provided by Geza Vermes, whose *Jesus the Jew* (1973) has probably been the greatest single influence in the field since Albert Schweitzer.[46]

And we should not forget that he is still seen by millions of Christians around the world in the way that St Paul, St Augustine, and Martin Luther saw him, and as the Pope and the present Archbishop of Canterbury see him now – as the inspired Son of God.

Here are some of the key questions that we have to answer if we are to understand, not just how Jesus was seen in his own times, but how he saw himself.

- Was his kingdom a heavenly one, or of this world?

- Was his mission to all humanity, or only to Jews?

- Was it for an infinite 'all time', or an approaching End Time?

- Did he will his own death, or was it a tragic accident?

- Did he die to wipe the slate clean, sacrificing himself for all mankind and redeeming 'the fall of Adam'?

- Did he rise from the dead?

- Was he God *and* Man, or only human?

These are sensitive and difficult questions. Our task here is simply to ask what light we can cast on them by a careful and detached study of the Gospels. To each question the Christ of faith answers yes (or chooses the first option). What would the Jesus of history have said?

My answers are based on two authors. Their work is entirely independent – neither refers to the other – and their religious views are not explicit in their work. One is Paula Fredriksen, particularly *From Jesus to Christ* and *Jesus of Nazareth, King of the Jews*. The other is Reza Aslan, author of *Zealot*. Both authors read the Gospels closely, almost as they would a detective story, looking for clues, for indications that all is not as it seems, for what is not said as well as what is. Aslan in particular looks at a number of anomalies in the way Jesus is described in the Gospels, and sets out to find an explanation that will make sense of them.

The first point he draws attention to is Jesus' repeated use of the terms 'Son of Man' and 'Kingdom of God'. Son of Man is used 81 times in the New Testament: 80 of those occurrences are in the Gospels (the remaining occasion is by Stephen, Acts 7:56). 'Kingdom of God' is likewise very restricted in its use, in this case almost entirely in Mark, the earliest Gospel. Both phrases have largely dropped out of the story of Christ but seem very important to the historical figure of Jesus.

The second point is Jesus' relentless criticism of the Jewish establishment: his praise of the poor, and his bitter condemnation of the rich Temple authorities. This is not simply the battle against the Pharisees – as we have seen, in Luke's Gospel relations with the Pharisees are quite good. If Jesus had been a simple Jewish nationalist, he would have turned his fire against the Roman occupiers. Why should he be so consistently opposed to the Jewish priestly establishment of the Temple?

Third is the way miracles are treated in the Gospels. Though Jesus is well able to perform such acts, he seems increasingly reluctant to do so. He insists that these actions are not just 'works of power' (the phrase used by writers of the time for such deeds), but also 'signs'. Signs of what?

Fourth is the importance Jesus attaches to the Twelve, a number that is sufficiently significant to be used both in the Gospels and in Acts, to the point where it is more important than the actual names of those chosen (which differ between the books of the New Testament).

Fifth – as we have seen – is the mysterious 'messianic secret', so prominent in Mark, and so much less evident in the later Gospels, as if a historical memory is preserved in the earliest account that becomes overwritten by the later theology.

The sixth anomaly, again one we have touched on already, is the striking (and universally accepted) fact that although Jesus was put to death by the authorities, *his followers were not*. If he was a threat to the authorities, why did they not act as they did with all the other would-be messiahs, and cut down his followers? And if he was not a threat, why was he executed at all?

The final point is one we have not touched on before. The teaching of Jesus as we have it in the Gospels is seen by those around him as quite surprising. John the Baptist preaches a recognisable message of repentance, and behaves in a recognisable way – solitary, self-denying, ascetic: as joggers like to say, 'No pain, no gain'. But Jesus' message, as it comes down to us, did not conform to any pattern that his hearers recognised. He obeyed the Law, but was relaxed about breaches of it; he performed miracles of healing, but did not insist on payment either in money or in repentance; he associated with the rural poor, but also with the urban rich; he lived a pure life, yet was not ashamed to keep company with drunks and prostitutes; his companions included numerous women and he seems to have treated them as equals. Not everything he says is gentle and forgiving; his yoke is not always easy nor his burden always light; yet if we look at what struck his contemporaries about his message, it is hard to find anywhere else in the Bible such a gentle, inclusive, and loving vision.

What identity, what kind of person, do these clues point to?

The Son of Man

Let us start with the mysterious references to 'the Son of Man'. This Aramaic phrase – it translates awkwardly into the Greek of the New Testament – can simply be a way of saying 'I', as in 'The fowls of the air have nests, but the Son of Man hath nowhere to lay his head'. But this definition will not cover every one of the 81 occasions where this phrase is used. In each of the Synoptic accounts of the trial, Jesus is asked if he is the messiah – but responds by deflecting the questions, insisting instead that he is 'the Son of Man' ('ho huios tou anthropou'): note 'the', not 'a'. This 'Son of Man' is unmistakeably the figure depicted in the second part of the prophetic Book of Daniel: 'Behold, one like the Son of Man came with the clouds of heaven, and came to the Ancient of Days [God] … And there was given him dominion, and glory, and a kingdom, that all people, nations, and languages, should serve him' (Daniel 7:13–14). At this crucial moment, Jesus is asked whether he sees himself as the messiah – a title with huge resonance for any Jew of that period – and emphatically insists that his preferred title is Son of Man. In Mark he even quotes Daniel directly: 'coming in the clouds of heaven' (Mark 14:62).

It seems, then, as though the Jesus of history – or at least the Jesus of the New Testament – saw himself, neither as God, nor as prophet, but as the figure appointed by God to restore Israel to its former glory and to install on earth the Kingdom of Heaven. This is the task of the Davidic messiah predicted in Zechariah: of a man who enters Jerusalem triumphant but also humble, powerful but also peaceful, and riding, not in the horse-drawn chariot of war, but on a donkey (Zechariah 9:9–10).

What kind of kingdom would this be? It would be unlike anything we know from history. It would be an ethical kingdom, living by the rules of the Sermon on the Mount; a just and equal one, in which the poor are blessed; a kingdom in which 'all things are possible' (Mark 10:27). And who better to rule it than the Son of Man as imagined by Mark's Jesus: a figure who is rejected (10:33) yet will judge (14:62), and who is both suffering servant (8:31, 10:45) and powerful ruler (8:38)?

What is the dominant quality of this kingdom? It is not independence. We are not looking at a simple freedom fighter. The essential ingredients are *zeal* and *love*. Love for one's fellow Jew: note that Leviticus 19:18, 'the golden rule', is not that one should love all men as oneself, but that one should love one's co-religionist in that way (which is why Jesus was so emphatic that he came to save 'the lost sheep of the house of Israel'). And zeal, pure passion, conviction, and courage, without which nothing can be achieved because Jesus does not dispose of any army. Zeal is the overwhelming power of the righteous – the pearl of great price, the readiness to sacrifice all that one has for righteousness and purity: 'Blessed are they which do hunger and thirst after righteousness: for they shall be filled' (Matthew 5:6). Zeal springs from the vision of the people of Israel living as they should; and zeal is offended by the sight of the Temple authorities living richly off the contributions of the poor.

There is evidence that social inequality was growing in Jesus' time and that the power and wealth of the priestly establishment was increasing. Jesus' target was not the Roman occupier, who couldn't be expected to know any better. His target was the great and the good of his own nation – who could. His miracles, like the NHS of our own times, were free at the point of delivery. Priestly healing was not. A leper made clean by a priest had to pay a considerable fee (including two birds and three lambs, Leviticus 14); Jesus and his disciples healed without charge. 'Heal the sick, cleanse the lepers, raise the dead, cast out devils: *freely ye have received, freely give*' (Matthew 10:8, emphasis added). When Jesus heals a leper and tells him to show himself to the priest and make an offering for his cleansing, he is highlighting the contrast between his own approach, and the greed of the priestly classes. Aslan suggests[47] that to Jesus' audience, the most striking feature of the parable of the Good Samaritan would not have been the goodness of the Samaritan, remarkable though that might be. It would have been the badness of the priest and the Levite.

How would the Kingdom of Heaven be established? We have referred earlier to the ambiguity of the New Testament attitude to violence. There is nothing in the Gospels to suggest that Jesus saw violence as his first recourse. But as we have seen earlier, there is plenty of evidence that he recognised that the use of force towards the Roman occupier might be a necessary price to pay.

Three texts are particularly telling here. Each is traditionally interpreted as a pointer to the spiritual, other-worldly nature of the kingdom; but there may be more than meets the eye.

When Jesus is asked the famous question about the Roman coin (Matthew 22:21, Luke 20:25), his answer is often given as 'Render' – in other words, 'Give' – 'to Caesar, that which is Caesar's'. But the Greek word is 'Apodidiomi' – 'Give back, restore to where it rightfully belongs', and the quotation continues, 'and [render] to God the things that are God's'. In other words, Caesar's coin should be restored to Caesar – *and what is God's, in other words the kingdom of Israel, should be restored to the people of Israel, its rightful owners.*

When Jesus instructs his followers to 'take up [your] cross, and follow me' (Matthew 16:24, Luke 9:23), we have learned to think of this as an invitation to self-sacrifice, to walk the Golgotha road. That is not what it would have meant to his audience. They knew that crucifixion was a political sentence – the punishment for rebellion. It is not a call to suffer: it is a call to become rebels.

Finally there is the enigmatic response to Pilate, 'My kingdom is not of this world' (John 18:36). My edition of the *New Oxford Annotated Bible* glosses this as 'the kingdom of Jesus is other-worldly, and no threat to Rome or Judea', and that is how it has been read in the past (not least because it is so consistent with the message of John's gospel). But many scholars – notably Rowan Williams, former Archbishop of Canterbury – read the Greek differently. Williams accepts an alternative translation, 'my kingdom is not of this sort' or 'not of this kind', and comments, 'this kind of royal authority is inseparable from the task, the calling, of embodying truth'.[48] If this is right, Jesus is not standing back from power and authority *in this world*: he is standing back from power and authority *of this kind*. What kind of kingdom would his be? The Kingdom of God – the one soon to be installed in Israel by the Son of Man, with its restored twelve tribes headed by the twelve apostles.

Let us turn now to the miracles – the signs and wonders that the Gospels record Jesus as having performed. The traditional way of seeing these is as good things in their own right: as love in action. If any of us had the capacity to heal blindness or epilepsy, or to feed the starving, would we not use it? And this is certainly one way in which Jesus uses his powers – out of kindness (Matthew 14:14 and 20:34, Mark 8:2, John 11:35 and 38, for example).

But it is puzzling that Jesus seems increasingly impatient, even irritable, with simply performing miracles. How can we explain this apparent 'compassion fatigue'? Reza Aslan convincingly suggests that 'his miracles are not intended as an end in themselves … they serve a pedagogical purpose. They are a means of conveying a very specific message to the Jews'.[49] The message is that the Kingdom of God that the Son of Man will usher in, *has already arrived*. When the followers of John the Baptist ask Jesus, 'Art thou he that should come, or do we look for another?', Jesus does not answer with a simple yes or no. He quotes from Isaiah 35:5–6 to show that the miracles are evidence of the actual presence of the Kingdom here and now: 'The blind receive their sight, and the lame walk, the lepers are cleansed, and the deaf hear, the dead are raised up, and the poor have the gospel preached to them' (Matthew 11:1–6, Luke 7:18–23: note the reference to 'the poor').

What of the Resurrection? The Resurrection is not just significant in itself: it is another sign that the End Time has arrived. 'I will open your graves', writes Ezekiel (37:12). So powerful is this belief that Matthew extends it beyond Jesus to others: 'And the graves were opened: and many bodies of the saints which slept arose' (Matthew 27:52). If we took this passage at its face value, we might expect that people who had been restored to life in this way would be brought forward to bear witness to the power of Jesus. In the event there is no further mention of them in the Gospel or in Acts.

Jesus' resurrection does not return him to normal life as if he had never died: that is not the point. Its symbolic importance is greater than its actual. As 'the first fruits of them that slept' (1 Corinthians 15:20), it demonstrates that other fruits will follow, that the Kingdom has arrived, the time when, as Daniel puts it, 'many of them that sleep in the dust of the earth shall awake' (Daniel 12:2).

Finally, what of the so-called Cleansing of the Temple, the turning over of the tables of the money-changers? Up till recently Bible scholars tended to accept the view of the Synoptics, that it was a very shocking and public event that provided the stimulus, the trigger, for the arrest and crucifixion of Jesus. But more recent commentators challenge this view. They point out that the Court of the Gentiles (the outer courtyard of the Temple) where the cleansing would have taken place was enormous (as big as a dozen football pitches) and would have accommodated tens of thousands, indeed hundreds of thousands, of pilgrims. To overturn a few

tables and release a few birds (the big animals were kept outside) would have been a trivial event, a minor scuffle far too
small to have had an impact on public opinion or to constitute
a challenge to the priesthood or to the Romans who guarded
the Temple precincts. But what if it did not symbolise cleansing, but destruction? The destruction and rebuilding of the
Temple is a recurring theme of Jewish apocalyptic writing – a
sign that the Kingdom of God is at hand.[50]

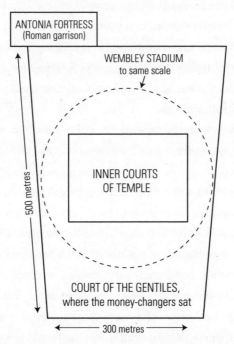

*Diagram 8. Herod's Temple in Jerusalem (started 20 BC, destroyed
by the Roman army 70 AD), the scene of Jesus overturning the
tables of the money-changers. For comparison, Wembley Stadium
(which seats 90,000) is shown to the same scale.*

These hints in the text point to a Jesus who believed him-self to be Daniel's Son of Man, the coming Saviour of the Jews. Such a Jesus would not himself be a danger, because the kingdom he preached would be brought about by act of God, not by force of arms. But the expectations placed upon him by the cheering Passover crowds made him a dangerous figure – not only to the Roman occupiers, but also to the wealthy priesthood, the 'theocracy' (as Josephus describes them) who controlled the revenues of the Temple.

If, as Paula Fredriksen suggests,[51] Jesus had 'lost control of his audience', it would not be surprising for the Jewish establishment to hand him over to the Romans for execution. But why did the Romans, contravening their usual policy, not pursue his followers also?

This is where the 'messianic secret' falls into place: the deliberate concealment of the miracles, and the deliberate obscurity of the parables, that is so pronounced in Mark. The evangelists told a story about a crucified and risen Son of God bringing salvation to mankind; they did not tell a story about Daniel's Son of Man, bringing in the Kingdom of Heaven on earth and restoring their rightful place to Jews, because Jesus had successfully concealed it from them, and not only from them but also from his disciples. Why did he do that? Because that was the only way in which he could protect them and ensure that when his own death came, he would not pull them down in the wreckage. As far as the Roman and the Temple authorities were concerned, Jesus was a prophet, a wonder worker, and a teacher; but (as John's account makes plain) they had seen him regularly in Jerusalem at Passover, and knew that he and his followers were harmless. This year the crowds got out of control, welcoming him as messiah and Son of David. That was too much; public order was threatened; he had to go. But there was no need to take his followers with him.

This account of the Jesus of history rests heavily on Reza Aslan's stimulating and closely argued *Zealot*. For all its originality – and the challenges it poses to orthodoxy – Aslan's account solves a number of puzzles, and builds elegantly on the work of other scholars.

And there is another reason why I think we should take Aslan's account seriously. The Christ of faith – Son of God, Maker of Heaven and Earth, Redeemer of Mankind, Vanquisher of Satan – is a wonderful creation, to be admired whether or not he is believed in. But we have to account for the fact that the Jesus of history was likewise a man loved and admired by his followers. The zealot pictured here (Aslan is at pains to point out that 'zealot' is with a small 'z', not the fully fledged Zealots of the political movement of 50–70 AD) – passionate, visionary, generous, and brave – would be a man worthy of such respect: of their respect, and of ours.

8. The New Testament: Conclusion

So – what conclusions can we draw from our examination of the New Testament?

We noted at the end of the first part of this book that the Old Testament is reliable neither as history, nor as a guide to action: it contains many facts and much teaching, but the reader has to choose which of those facts, and which of those teachings, to accept. The same message emerges from a close reading of the New Testament. What Jesus had to say about the good life – though inspirational – often contradicts what is taught elsewhere in the New Testament, and sometimes indeed what Jesus himself says. The Bible can be used to support many different positions and teachings, but it cannot tell us how to choose between them. We have to do that ourselves.

To that conclusion I would add two further points that have stood out for me. The first is the enormous importance of the Jewish roots of Christianity. The New Testament is built upon the Old Testament; the prophets of Judaism – Abraham, Moses, Elijah – are the patriarchs of Christianity; the law that Jesus commends to his followers is the Torah of Judaism; the actions of Jesus are constantly accounted for as having been 'foretold by the Scriptures', those very Scriptures that form the largest part of the two-book Christian Bible. It is not too much to call Christianity a subset of Judaism.

And this is not just a formal link, a kind of historical courtesy. The core values of the New Testament are closely aligned with the values and the worldview of the Old Testament prophets. The contexts and metaphors are drawn from a rural world of farmers and shepherds, of ploughing, sowing, harvesting, fishing, caring for flocks, sweeping and cleaning. The life of the rich is not a matter of stocks and shares or a cohort of bodyguards, but of a householder sitting up all night to protect his own possessions from thieves; the loss of a single silver piece (Luke 15:8–10) is a disaster. And just as the New Testament is egalitarian and suspicious of any kind of hierarchy, so it is suspicious of any kind of wealth: the poor and the meek are singled out for blessing, not just in the Gospels, but in Acts and the Epistles too. The apostles are poor men with little education; the communities of early Christians in Acts and the Epistles are for the most part made up of the marginalised – the working class, women, aliens, the underprivileged. And the disciples behave like the Old Testament prophets in 'speaking truth to power', in challenging the authorities, not in the name of rebellion, but – like Elijah and Nathan before them – in the name of justice.

Consistent with this simple and rustic framework is the emphasis in Judaism on the enjoyment of life. Jesus was not out of step with the prophets in his readiness to eat, drink, and be merry: it was the puritanical John the Baptist who was the exception.

And the Christianity of the New Testament, like the Judaism of the Old Testament, was an intensely communal religion. With the exception of the very small group of the Essenes, the Jews had no tradition of monasticism, no 'examen de conscience' intended to turn the individual believer's gaze inward to his or her soul. The repeated calls to repentance of the Old Testament prophets, like the later call from John the Baptist, are not accusations addressed to individual hearers charging them with being lazy, dishonest, or uncharitable. They are accusations to the audience *en masse* of disobedience to God – primarily shown in a failure to observe and reflect on the Torah – and a forgetfulness of their sacred purpose as a people: to be the chosen ones of God. And like its Jewish source, early Christianity was not an individualistic religion; it was concerned with practice and above all with obedience – obedience to the teaching of Jesus, and behind that obedience to the will of God.

Finally, as we saw with the Old Testament, it was a religion of community in the sense of communal responsibility. Communal responsibility explains why the sins of the fathers shall be visited upon the children, why 'The fathers have eaten a sour grape, and the children's teeth are set on edge' (Jeremiah 31:29). But it also explains the fellowship and social responsibility enjoined upon the community of believers in Acts, the rule that they should take care of each other, look after the widows and orphans, and practise compassion as the greatest of all virtues.

Scholars have noted the popularity of the synagogues in the Classical world and it is not hard to see the appeal of Judaism when compared to an increasingly directionless and rootless set of pagan beliefs. Judaism offered a deep theology available in a Greek translation; a welcoming and joyful attitude to life; simple, unthreatening social attitudes that did not exclude 'the great unwashed'; and above all a strong moral and ethical message of responsibility for one's fellow man.

And if Judaism offered this – so did Christianity. For these Old Testament values are exactly mirrored in the New.

We have seen the challenge faced by Christianity of severing the umbilical cord binding it to its Jewish parent (one is

reminded of the agonising task of separating Siamese twins).
Nor was it only Jews and Christians who found the relationship confusing: throughout the 1st century AD and beyond
there was a tendency to assume that Christians 'were' Jews,
and that Jewish communities should be held accountable for
the behaviour of Christian believers.

This would be difficult enough at the best of times –
but there was an added complication. We know from Acts
of the energy (and success) of Christian missionary activity among both Jews and Gentiles, and of the problems it
caused. But there is a strand missing from Acts, highlighted by
19th-century historians, which has dropped out of the debate
until recently. For a number of years it has been assumed that
Second-Temple Judaism, the faith of Jesus and his contemporaries, was an exclusive belief and did not allow conversion
except in very rare circumstances. It is increasingly clear that
this is not the case. *The Judaism of Jesus' time was also a missionary faith bent on making converts – and highly successful at doing so.*

We know that the number of practising Jews increased
enormously in the centuries before the birth of Jesus: from
Babylon and Persia in the East, all round the Mediterranean,
and eastwards to Alexandria and beyond. This cannot be
explained by any other means than by conversion. The
Hebrew Bible was translated into Greek in the 2nd century
BC; we know both from their writings and from records of
surnames that there were numerous Jews outside Palestine
who were converts rather than émigrés and who simply did
not speak Hebrew.

Some of this conversion was peaceful and voluntary, through the synagogues and the process of 'God-fearers' becoming Jews. Some of it certainly was not. Around 125 BC Israel under the Hasmonean dynasty conquered their old enemy Edom and forced the population to be circumcised and accept the faith; in 103 BC the same process was repeated for Galilee – soon to be the home of Jesus – and its Iturean inhabitants (a fact that casts a tantalising shadow across the long genealogies of Jesus cited in Matthew and Luke). Whatever the method, in the time of Jesus great Jewish writers such as Philo of Alexandria (who spoke no Hebrew) and Josephus were aiming their writings at the conversion of Gentiles, and over the next 500 years Judaism as a religion was adopted by whole populations in the Caucasus, in North Africa, in Iberia, in the Arabian peninsula (where it profoundly influenced the subsequent development of Islam) and in Ethiopia, where recent DNA evidence has confirmed that 'Beta Israel' – the 80–90,000 Ethiopian Jews airlifted to Israel in the 1980s – are primarily from the Ethiopian rather than the Mediterranean gene pool.

As the great 19th-century historian Theodor Mommsen put it: 'Ancient Judaism was not exclusive at all; it was, rather, as keen to propagate itself as Christianity and Islam would be in future.'[52]

This is of profound importance for relations with early Christian missionaries. The synagogues that sprang up around the Mediterranean in the late Classical period were not just places of worship for Jews and of cultural outreach – like

British Council reading rooms – for God-fearing pagans. They were recruitment centres for Judaism, and very busy and effective ones too. Consequently it is not hard to imagine the effect when a new wave of preachers arrived in the synagogue, not aiming to support the Jewish mission, but criticising Judaism and offering instead to the pool of potential converts in the congregation a new faith with all the advantages of Judaism and without the painful ordeal of circumcision – a kind of 'Judaism Lite'. It is scarcely surprising that Paul and his fellows were not well received; they would have been about as welcome as an Avon lady at a Tupperware party.

I said earlier that two things had stood out for me from the process of working on the New Testament. The first, as we have seen, is the Jewishness of Christianity. The second is the extraordinary distance from the first disciples to the established churches of today: from Galilee, so to speak, to Rome. The angry prophet from Nazareth; the wandering life from village to village; the rough, witty Aramaic sayings; the humble, rural occupations – fishermen, shepherds, carpenters – of the disciples who heard Jesus' message and proclaimed it day by day in the Temple; the profound distrust and resentment felt by the Gospel writers for the rich … all that is so different from the way that Christianity developed on its Hellenising route westwards from Nazareth to Rome and to recognition, influence, and finally in the 4th century to power as the established Church of the Roman Empire. It feels a long way from Jesus to Christ.

PART THREE

A VISION OF FREEDOM

'The Bible is clearly a major element in our own imaginative tradition, whatever we may think we believe about it. It insistently raises the question: Why does this huge, sprawling, tactless book sit there inscrutably in the middle of our cultural heritage […] frustrating all our efforts to walk round it?'

(H. Northrop Frye, *The Great Code: the Bible and Literature*, 1981, pp. xviii–xix)

1. Is there a different way to read the Bible?

The first two parts of this book have set out to show that the Bible has very little correspondence with historical reality, and that its laws and commandments cannot be made to constitute a coherent 'instruction manual' for the conduct of life. In a nutshell, I have argued that every attempt at a 'literal' or 'fundamentalist' reading of the Bible is – to borrow a very Biblical phrase – built on sand.

One way in which we might gain a different perspective would be to take some episodes from the Bible and look at them from a purely literary standpoint: to examine them through the lens we use for imaginative fiction, and to consider the techniques they use, and the impact they create, in a way entirely independent of their faith content or their truth content. If we land on the desert island with just the Bible and Shakespeare – can we read the Bible in the same way that we read Shakespeare?

This turns out to be not merely a rhetorical question. The difficulty becomes clear when we consider three sentences.

a) 'Confronted with Claudius kneeling in prayer, Hamlet exercises restraint'

b) 'Confronted with Eve's persuasion, Adam is unable to resist'

c) 'Confronted with Gabriel's message, Mary humbly accepts'

The first sentence (adapted from Mark Rose's *Shakespearean Design*) is unlikely to cause us any difficulty: I do not expect letters from readers pointing out to me that Hamlet and Claudius are fictional characters. But the second and third (of my own devising) are increasingly problematic. In the modern world, there is a broad consensus that Genesis is a metaphor rather than an account of real events, so I may be allowed to get away with talking about Adam and Eve without seeming to assert that they actually exist. But what if I speak about Gabriel and Mary? To write about their characters and actions feels somehow different, as if we were affirming the reality of their existence, in a way that we would not feel if we wrote of (say) Madame Bovary, or James Bond, or Paddington Bear.

So I must make a strong plea to my readers here. I began this book with the assertion that the argument it puts forward neither requires, nor precludes, belief: it is about the Bible, not about faith. I will repeat that here. In the remainder of this section I shall write about, and attempt to analyse and explore, a number of Biblical episodes and characters. This is, as the lawyers say, 'without prejudice': I wish neither to assert the historical and theological truth of the events I shall write about, nor to deny it. All I can ask of the reader is to reverse the famous Coleridge phrase, and to be ready for the next few pages to make 'a willing suspension of belief'.

Nor is this the only difficulty we encounter when we try to write about sacred texts. The 'register' of everyday language – the kind of words and phrases that we use, the rhythm of our speech – is quite different from the register of sacred language. 'First up, God put the whole lot together' is in one way the same as 'In the beginning God created heaven and earth', but in another way it is quite different; how it is said is as important as what is said. The language of formal occasions reminds us of this: the best man's speech at the wedding is as rule-governed as the marriage service, but those rules are very different from each other. The difficulty is that *as secular language becomes more serious, it progressively and inevitably comes to sound more like sacred language.* The words and rhythms of the Gettysburg address, of Churchill's wartime speeches, of Roosevelt's two inaugural addresses, of Shakespeare's tragic final speeches, were not written and spoken for religious occasions or for religious purposes, yet they use the techniques that we associate with religion. And that is as it should be. High seriousness is a part of these solemn secular occasions as much as it is a part of the solemnities of religion. More brides go down the aisle to Gloria Gaynor's 'I Will Survive' than to any other tune (though it seems doubtful that they have fully taken in the words of the rest of the song): it may be only a piece of rock music, but the resonance with the Psalms has not escaped them.

Language – whether sacred or secular – inspires us; it thrills us; it moves us. Emily Dickinson said, 'When I feel physically as though the top of my head had been taken off, I know that is poetry'. The high seriousness of secular oratory can sound and feel very like the high solemnity of religious conviction. Anyone who examines religious language is going to find that it evokes feelings of solemnity and awe. The grandeur of the opening verses of Genesis; the iambic rhythms and variations of God's covenant with Noah ('While the earth remaineth, seed-time and harvest, and cold and heat, and summer and winter, and day and night shall not cease', Genesis 8:22); the way the Psalms ('They that go down to the sea in ships, that do business in great waters', 107:23, 'Out of the depths have I cried unto thee, O Lord', 130:1) dignify and ennoble the everyday activities and griefs of daily life; the deep insights of the Epistles ('But the greatest of these is love'); the measured redundancies of the Prayer Book ('to have and to hold', 'dust to dust', 'man that is born of woman') – all these, like the secular writings of the paragraph before, are expressions of human seriousness wrought to its highest pitch. Poetic inspiration is hard to tell from religious inspiration. For our purposes here I shall make no distinction between the secular and the sacred.

This preamble is important because I want to choose a few passages from the Bible to show the extraordinary variety and power of its writing. I am aware that I will be quoting these texts, and analysing them, in translation, but this is the way they have come down to us in the Western world – whether the Greek into which the original authors rendered the words of Jesus, or Jerome's 4th-century Latin, or the 1611 Authorised Version that we are using here. I shall use it because the trans-lators deliberately matched style to content, and did not shy away from the heightened language suited to all seriousness, whether sacred or secular. I was tempted to start with the first chapter of Genesis but have decided not to because I have already commented on it at some length in Part One. Instead

I would like to examine three passages – one from the Old Testament, two from the New – where the religious intensity may be less, and yet the literary qualities are as great. I will begin with a story from the Book of Samuel.

2. Three Bible passages: a literary appreciation

1. David, Bathsheba, and the ewe lamb (2 Samuel 11 and 12)
The first passage we shall consider is David's seduction of Bathsheba, his murder of her husband, and the response of the prophet Nathan.

The figure of David towers over Old and New Testaments alike. In the Old Testament he rises from a humble background to become the ruler who triumphantly unites the northern and southern kingdoms and defeats their foes in a series of bloody battles. More importantly, he establishes a special relationship with God which ensures that the throne will always belong to the house and lineage of David: while the penalty of his sins may be visited on him and on his descendants, their right to rule will never be taken away. This is of course why Jesus has to be descended from David and born in Bethlehem, 'the city of David'.

This passage is taken from the so-called 'Court Histories' written in the northern kingdom between about 840 and 722 BC, making it the oldest of the major strands of Old Testament writing. We have met the author before: he (or she – see page 54) is the writer of the story of the Garden of Eden in Genesis 2.

When the passage begins, David has established his rule over both Israel and Judah. He has sent his troops to war, led by his faithful nephew and 'fixer' Joab; for unexplained reasons, David remains behind in Jerusalem.

2. And it came to pass in an evening-tide, that David arose from off his bed, and walked upon the roof of the king's house: and from the roof he saw a woman washing herself; and the woman was very beautiful to look upon.

3. And David sent and enquired after the woman. And one said, Is not this Bathsheba, the daughter of Eliam, the wife of Uriah the Hittite?

4. And David sent messengers, and took her; and she came in unto him, and he lay with her; for she was purified from her uncleanness: and she returned to her house.

5. And the woman conceived, and sent and told David, and said, I am with child.

6. And David sent to Joab, saying, Send me Uriah the Hittite. And Joab sent Uriah to David.

7. And when Uriah was come unto him, David demanded of him how Joab did, and how the people did, and how the war prospered.

8. And David said to Uriah, Go down to thy house, and wash thy feet. And Uriah departed out of the king's house, and there followed him a mess of meat from the king.

9. But Uriah slept at the door of the king's house with all the servants of his lord, and went not down to his house.

10. And when they had told David, saying, Uriah went not down unto his house, David said unto Uriah, Camest thou not from thy journey? why then didst thou not go down unto thine house?

11. And Uriah said unto David, The ark, and Israel, and Judah, abide in tents: and my lord Joab, and the servants of my lord, are encamped in the open fields: shall I then go into mine house, to eat and to drink, and to lie with my wife? as thou livest, and as thy soul liveth, I will not do this thing.

12. And David said to Uriah, Tarry here today also, and tomorrow I will let thee depart. So Uriah abode in Jerusalem that day, and the morrow.

13. And when David had called him, he did eat and drink before him: and he made him drunk: and at even he went out to lie on his bed with the servants of his lord, but went not down to his house.

14. And it came to pass in the morning, that David wrote a letter to Joab, and sent it by the hand of Uriah.

15. And he wrote in the letter, saying, Set ye Uriah in the forefront of the hottest battle, and retire ye from him, that he may be smitten, and die.

16. And it came to pass, when Joab observed the city, that he assigned Uriah unto a place where he knew that valiant men were.

17. And the men of the city went out, and fought with Joab: and there fell some of the people of the servants of David; and Uriah the Hittite died also.

18. Then Joab sent and told David all the things concerning the war;

19. And charged the messenger, saying, When thou hast made an end of telling the matters of the war unto the king,

20. And if so be that the king's wrath arise, and he say unto thee, Wherefore approached ye so nigh unto the city when ye did fight? knew ye not that they would shoot from the wall?

21. Who smote Abimelech the son of Jerubbesheth? did not a woman cast a piece of a millstone upon him from the wall, that he died in Thebez? why went ye nigh the wall? then say thou, Thy servant Uriah is dead also.

22. So the messenger went, and came and shewed David all that Joab had sent him for.

23. And the messenger said unto David, Surely the men prevailed against us, and came out unto us into the field, and we were upon them even unto the entering of the gate.

24. And the shooters shot from off the wall upon thy servants; and some of the king's servants be dead, and thy servant Uriah the Hittite is dead also.

25. Then David said unto the messenger, Thus shalt thou say unto Joab, Let not this thing displease thee, for the sword devoureth one as well as another: make thy battle more strong against the city, and overthrow it: and encourage thou him.

26. And when the wife of Uriah heard that Uriah her husband was dead, she mourned for her husband.

27. And when the mourning was past, David sent and fetched her to his house, and she became his wife, and bare

him a son. But the thing that David had done displeased the Lord.

Chapter 12

1. And the Lord sent Nathan unto David. And he came unto him, and said to him, There were two men in one city; the one rich, and the other poor.

2. The rich man had exceeding many flocks and herds:

3. But the poor man had nothing, save one little ewe lamb, which he had bought and nourished up: and it grew up together with him, and with his children; it did eat of his own meat, and drank of his own cup, and lay in his bosom, and was unto him as a daughter.

4. And there came a traveller unto the rich man, and he spared to take of his own flock and of his own herd, to dress for the wayfaring man that was come unto him; but took the poor man's lamb, and dressed it for the man that was come to him.

5. And David's anger was greatly kindled against the man; and he said to Nathan, As the Lord liveth, the man that hath done this thing shall surely die;

6. And he shall restore the lamb fourfold, because he did this thing, and because he had no pity.

7. And Nathan said to David, Thou art the man.

(2 Samuel 11 and 12)

The passage begins with a carefully painted image: the naked form of a woman seen on a rooftop, lit by the glow of a setting sun. (We note that King David lives in a house – the glory days of Solomon's splendid palace are far ahead.) David, struck by her beauty, enquires and finds out her name. Bathsheba is of Hebrew ancestry, and married; her husband's name is also Hebrew, but he is described as 'the Hittite', marking him as a resident alien, a category under the special protection of the kings of Israel; moreover we learn later that Uriah is one of David's 30 best soldiers (2 Samuel 23:39). Despite this, David sends for Bathsheba and lies with her. The text reveals that Bathsheba had been menstruating – hence the washing – and that her period was now over ('she was purified from her uncleanness', 11:4; see Leviticus 15:19–28: David may have broken a moral law against adultery, but he was careful not to break the purity laws governing the timing of sexual intercourse). Consequently Bathsheba is at her most fertile, and she duly conceives (11:5).

The second part (11:6–13) of this curiously ruthless passage recounts David's efforts to bring Bathsheba's husband back from the front line, so that husband can sleep with wife and in due course believe himself to be the father of David's child. David sends for Uriah: Joab, unquestioning as ever, complies. After some royal small talk about conditions at the front (11:7), Uriah is sent home to have a candle-lit dinner with his wife ('there followed him a mess of meat', 11:8) and then 'wash his feet' (11:7), 'feet' in both Old and New Testaments being a standard euphemism for genitals. But Uriah is made of sterner stuff and will not betray his comrades in arms, preferring to stay with the men of David's household. As he says to

David when challenged, 'The ark, and Israel, and Judah' – the twin kingdoms that David had so recently united – 'abide in tents … shall I then go into mine house, to eat and to drink, and to lie with my wife?' (11:11). David has one more try by getting Uriah drunk, but Uriah's loyalty and decency are unshaken; he will not go home to Bathsheba.

So David arranges for Uriah's death, making Uriah himself unwittingly deliver his own death warrant (11:14–21). Joab loyally fixes that also. Unfortunately not all goes quite to plan, and some other soldiers are killed as well as Uriah. Joab is anxious about how David might react to these unintended casualties and prudently counsels the messenger how to win the king over. The plan works: before David can query the deaths, the messenger adroitly points out that 'thy servant Uriah the Hittite is dead also' (11:24); David's wrath is averted and he responds philosophically that 'the sword devoureth one as well as another', bearing out La Rochefoucauld's wise maxim that we are all strong enough to bear the troubles of others.

David's stratagem has succeeded, but 'the thing that David had done displeased the Lord' (11:27), and the prophet Nathan is enlisted to bring this displeasure to the notice of the king. Nathan and David know each other of old, but the commission is still a tricky one, trapping the prophet between the rock of God and the hard place of the king's displeasure. It would not be the only time in the Book of Samuel when a messenger was literally killed (2 Samuel 1:15). Nathan finds the elegant solution of recasting the events in fictional form, as the story of a rich man (the 'he' of 12:4) who refuses to take from his own 'exceeding many flocks and herds' to feed his guest, but instead kills and serves the poor man's beloved lamb. His tale holds up a mirror to David: if the king gets the point, he will condemn himself, thus avoiding the necessity for Nathan to make the risky challenge. The plan works. David judges himself unawares, and the trap is sprung with the fatal words, 'Thou art the man'.*

What is it that makes this relevant to our purposes here? First, I think, its interest in character. Under the smooth surface of the narrative lie taut sinews of motivation: David's calculations as to how to avoid a paternity suit, Uriah's decent refusal to take a comfort denied to his fellows at the front line, Joab's careful spinning of the bad military news, Nathan's ingenious device to avoid the royal wrath. Even Bathsheba herself may be less of an innocent victim than at first appears: was she completely unaware that David's roof overlooked hers? Was she perhaps 'no better than she should be', nurturing a cunning plan to insert herself into the royal lineage, as she did in due course as the mother of Solomon? There is not only a novelist's eye for character and situation, but a novelist's ear for conversational detail: the small talk of 11:7, the carefully edited bulletin from the front line (11:24), and David's bland, political response (11:25).

---

* This is even pithier in the Latin translation of the Vulgate: 'De te fabula', 'the story is about you'.

THREE BIBLE PASSAGES: A LITERARY APPRECIATION

Secondly there is the recognition of human imperfection and of the breadth and depth of human experience lived within a single character. On the one hand David is the king '[whose] throne shall be established for ever' (7:16); on the other he is the man who embarrasses his wife with his undignified dancing in public (2 Samuel 6:16) and who contrives the death of a sexual rival. David knows the heights but also the depths: he knows the pride and the power of kingship and the bitter despair of the loss of his friend Jonathan and his son Absalom.

Third is the way the J writer uses the technique of dramatic irony. Irony – from the Greek 'eiron' – is originally the technique of understatement, of words that imply more than they actually say. Dramatic irony – typically of course in a drama – is when the reader, or the audience, has information that the character(s) do not. As Nathan speaks, the reader starts to make the connections that David misses. This story is not going to be about sheep! Dramatic irony is most famous in Greek drama of the 5th century BC, and presupposes a sophisticated writer and a responsive audience. Here we find it three centuries before Sophocles.

But perhaps the most striking aspect of this whole passage is the relationship – and the distinction – between truth and power. Despite the great distance between heaven and earth in the Old Testament, and the unconditional authority that God wields over his chosen people, there is an extraordinary tradition of independence and even resistance running alongside. Abraham bargains with God over the destruction of

Sodom (Genesis 18); Moses begs God to deliver him from the burden that the same God has put upon him; Jonah grumbles against God's refusal to annihilate Nineveh as he had promised to do. And the challenging mirror that Nathan holds up to the mighty David is one more sign of the readiness of individuals in the Old Testament to tell it like it is and not toe the party line – to speak truth to power. The Old Testament writers respected not only the power of their God, but the dogged individualism of their human characters. Job, crushed and pounded into the dust by the wrath of God, still insists that 'Though he slay me … I will maintain mine own ways before him' (Job 13:15).

2: Luke's Nativity (Luke 2:1–19)

The next passage that I want to examine is Luke's account of the Nativity. I would ask the reader, before turning the page, to call to mind what they remember of the Christmas story. If they are anything like me, the overall impression is atmospheric and moving, but the detail is a little confused: a jumble of candle-lit memories – Midnight Mass, the Nine Lessons and Carols, the school Nativity play – and an assortment of images: the star, the Wise Men, the manger, the shepherds, the animals. Somewhere, you feel, there must be a camel. Oh yes, and the Slaughter of the Innocents: and haven't I seen a picture of Mary on a donkey holding the baby, on her way somewhere?

This collection of images, and the story that connects them, is brought to life for us (or done to death) every year. The structure behind the annunciation and birth of Jesus is a very old one, connecting it to many stories about the birth of a quasi-divine hero. In such tales – frequent in Classical mythology because of Zeus' fondness for human women – there is typically a real father who is a king or a god and seeks to harm the child out of jealousy, and human foster-parents (often shepherds) who protect the child. That is the story of Oedipus, sentenced to death by his own parents; the birth of Dionysus, well known in Mediterranean mystery religions, presents another version. Often, as in *Daphnis and Chloe* or in the story of Gawain, there are birth tokens placed beside the abandoned child that later prove its special parentage: the gifts of the kings to the infant Jesus are examples of this, reminding us of the kingly nature of this apparently humble child. A displaced form of the same plot is recognisable in the stories of Moses, where the role of the jealous father is transferred to Pharaoh, and of course of Jesus himself, where the jealous father is played by Herod. Moses, floating in the bulrushes, is saved through the quick wits of his mother and sister and eventually escapes from Egypt: Jesus' human father Joseph reverses the stratagem and saves the child by fleeing into Egypt.

In terms of the New Testament, however, it is fascinating to realise on what a narrow foundation this compelling story rests. Mark, the first evangelist, and John, the last, have nothing to say about the birth of Jesus: the accounts in Matthew and Luke cannot be squared with each other. I will focus here on the account provided by Luke.

Unlike Matthew, who starts in with the genealogy of Jesus and leads straight on from that to his birth, Luke prepares his account with a number of framing devices so that we shall have a proper understanding of the significance of what he describes. He begins with four verses (already quoted) addressed to Theophilus in which he sets out his stall as a serious historian writing 'That thou mightest know the certainty of those things' (Luke 1:3–4). Thereafter he interweaves two stories of miraculous births – John the Baptist, and Jesus. He starts with a very detailed account of the circumstances surrounding the birth of John the Baptist, born 'in the days of Herod, the King of Judea' to parents of impeccable priestly pedigree. The coming birth of John is announced to his parents-to-be with a judicious blend of precise detail – the angel stands 'on the right side of the altar of incense' – and mythical depth: Elisabeth the mother is barren, Zacharias the father is 'well stricken in years', and the angel strikes Zacharias dumb 'because thou believest not my words' – an action that echoes the reproof of the angel to Sarah and Abraham in Genesis (18:9–15).*

It is clear from this that something of high importance is afoot, and the task foretold for John the Baptist – 'to make ready a people prepared for the Lord' – matches the special circumstances of his birth. The story then moves up a gear with Gabriel's visit a few months later to Mary of Nazareth, a cousin of Elisabeth, in order to tell her that she will give birth

---

* For other births to supposedly barren women see Rebekah in Genesis 25:21–26, Rachel in Genesis 29:31 and 30:22–24, and the mother of Samson in Judges 13:2–5.

in a still more mysterious fashion (she is still a virgin) to a child whose destiny is even greater than that of John. John, the one who '[shall] go before the face of the Lord to prepare his ways' (Luke 1:76), is duly born to great and prayerful rejoicing. The warm-up is over: the stage is set for the appearance of Jesus.

1. And it came to pass in those days, that there went out a decree from Caesar Augustus, that all the world should be taxed.

2. (And this taxing was first made when Cyrenius was governor of Syria.)

3. And all went to be taxed, every one into his own city.

4. And Joseph also went up from Galilee, out of the city of Nazareth, into Judaea, unto the city of David, which is called Bethlehem; (because he was of the house and lineage of David:)

5. To be taxed with Mary his espoused wife, being great with child.

6. And so it was, that, while they were there, the days were accomplished, that she should be delivered.

7. And she brought forth her firstborn son, and wrapped him in swaddling clothes, and laid him in a manger; because there was no room for them in the inn.

8. And there were in the same country shepherds abiding in the field, keeping watch over their flock by night.

9. And, lo, the angel of the Lord came upon them, and the glory of the Lord shone round about them: and they were sore afraid.

10. And the angel said unto them, Fear not: for behold, I bring you good tidings of great joy, which shall be to all people.

11. For unto you is born this day in the city of David a Saviour, which is Christ the Lord.

12. And this shall be a sign unto you: Ye shall find the babe wrapped in swaddling clothes, lying in a manger.

13. And suddenly there was with the angel a multitude of the heavenly host praising God, and saying,

14. Glory to God in the highest, and on earth peace, good will toward men.

15. And it came to pass, as the angels were gone away from them into heaven, the shepherds said one to another, Let us go now even unto Bethlehem, and see this thing which is come to pass, which the Lord hath made known to us.

16. And they came with haste, and found Mary, and Joseph, and the babe lying in a manger.

17. And when they had seen it, they made known abroad the saying which was told them concerning the child.

18. And all they that heard it wondered at those things which were told them by the shepherds.

19. But Mary kept all those things, and pondered them in her heart.

(Luke 2:1–19)

A striking feature of this passage is the frequency of 'And': fifteen of the nineteen verses begin with it. These are words written to be spoken (not surprising given that the Authorised

Version was 'appointed to be read [aloud]'), with a cumulative power, like a succession of breaking waves, which neither offers nor requires explanation. The only explanatory passages are those bracketed off in verses 2 and 4, where – as we shall see in a moment – Luke is laying the historical and bureaucratic groundwork for the mysteries that follow.

To begin his account Luke adopts his official-historian style, appropriate for references to government and to taxation. The wheels of state are set in motion: 'it came to pass' confers a sense of predestined and dignified inevitability, and the reference to Caesar Augustus places the events that follow in their world-historical framework and sets up the public side of a contrast that we will return to later. The reference to that particular Caesar is not merely historical, however: it has a literary purpose also, evoking in the reader of the time associations of mild and benevolent kingship. The reign of Caesar Augustus (27 BC–14 AD) marked, in the wider Roman Empire for which Luke was writing, a time of such calm and tranquillity that it was known as the 'pax augusta'.

The historical context narrows and focuses, from the Roman Empire, to Syria, to Galilee, from 'all' to 'Joseph', and from Joseph, to Mary, to the child. It moves from the measured progress of the events and processes of state – 'it came to pass', 2:1 – to the equally measured progress and process of pregnancy and birth: 'the days were accomplished, that she should be delivered', 2:6.

And just as Mary and Joseph have no choice about where to go to be taxed, so Mary has no choice about where to lay the newborn baby. If you haven't got a room, you take what's going: a stable will have to do.

Those first seven verses, with their steady onward movement, their *Just So Stories* echoes of storytelling ('in those days', 'it came to pass', 'and so it was'), and their precisely judged phrasing (note the semi-colon after 'manger' in verse 7, forcing the reader to pause so as not to miss the significance of what precedes and follows it) – these are beautifully crafted.*

But we must also draw attention to two crucial words in verse 7: 'firstborn', and 'manger'.

'Firstborn' is not simply there as a clinical or a genealogical term. Of course any mother's firstborn might be expected to have unique significance for her. But for the attentive reader, 'firstborn' is a word loaded with significance. Being firstborn is a risky place in the Bible. The Lord has a special claim on firstborns ('all the firstborn are mine', Numbers 3:13). The firstborn of Egypt were killed at the first Passover, the first-born often lose out to their younger brother (Esau to Jacob, Cain – initially – to Abel), and there is a dark tradition running through the Old Testament of sacrificing the eldest child (Abraham and Isaac, Jephthah and his daughter, and numerous references to Moloch and Canaanite gods). And what is true for humans is true for animals too. Leviticus instructs that

* As mentioned above, I am aware that the Authorised Version text analysed here is a translation from the original Greek. The structure of the story is Luke's, but credit for the punctuation goes to Benjamin Blayney's 1769 revision of the 1611 translation.

the firstborn of domestic animals are to be sacrificed. Sheep are also mothers and doubtless feel the same aching tenderness for their firstborn: but whether animal or human, little creatures that are born in stables and outhouses, laid on straw, and watched over by shepherds, can seldom look forward to a long life.

So 'firstborn' calls up a number of poignant associations. What of 'manger'? Luke uses this term on two levels. The first is a symbol of exclusion, a marker of poverty and humility that unites the King of the Jews with the poorest of his subjects. But the manger also links the human world with the animal world, making this birth an event intended to resonate, not just with all humanity, but with all the living world and hence with all creation. It cannot be by accident that Luke has so structured his story that apart from the parents the first living creatures to see the baby are not Wise Men or kings, not prophets or scholars, but humble beasts of burden.

Every Christmas crib scene has an ox and an ass. There is no mention of these in Luke, but the Church quickly moved to fill the gap and the earliest pictorial representations show the crib watched over by these two animals.* The attraction has not faded, as is shown by the Hardy poem quoted in a previous section and the tradition that it refers to of the animals kneeling on Christmas Eve. Whatever the Scripture says or does not say, the reader's unconscious feels the pull: if there is

---

* The justification often claimed by reference to Isaiah 1:3 is entirely without foundation.

a manger, there must be animals, ready to surround the child of a loving God with their own unconditional devotion.

Finally Luke's regard for women is evident in the grammar of verse 7, where it is Mary, and not Joseph or the baby, who is placed at the centre of the action and who is the subject of all the first three verbs.

Verses 1–7 brought us to the birth. Verses 8–18 introduce new protagonists. The choice of shepherds is hugely significant and suggestive. Shepherds look after sheep – and in that they follow the example of God ('The Lord is my shepherd', Psalm 23), and foreshadow Jesus himself ('I am the good shepherd', John 10:11). Shepherds keep watch, as the first disciples failed to do at Gethsemane, and as the later disciples were enjoined to do by the writers of the early Epistles. And shepherds represent the humble and meek, part of the 'all people' to whom the good tidings are brought (2: 10), for whom the Saviour is born (2:11), and who receive the 'good will' of the angels (2:14).

The language follows this through with a beautiful subtlety: 'came to pass', with its sense of solemn fulfilment, is picked up from verse 1 and repeated twice in verse 15. The shepherds travel to Bethlehem* and there they see, first Mary (as we would expect from Luke!), then Joseph, and finally the baby, shown first, and before all others, to these working men. The cadences and rhythms of the text – the way the

---

* The Authorised Version's 'came' in 2:16 is so much more immediate, so much more evocative of homecoming, than the 'went' of the New Revised Standard Version.

angels fade away like fireworks against the night sky, or the carefully placed commas of verse 16 – are perfectly calculated to support the atmosphere that pervades the passage, a sense, not of the remoteness and awe of the Old Testament, but of something more intimate that the New Revised Standard Version calls 'amazement' but the Authorised Version, more sensitively, 'wonder'.

Finally there is the one-verse conclusion, the response of Mary – significantly introduced with 'But' rather than the familiar 'And' (2:19). The story began with Caesar Augustus: it ends with a girl in a stable. It is a conclusion that marks a movement, over the whole nineteen verses, from exalted to humble; from public to private; from official to personal; from outer to inner. As so often, Luke gives the last word – or more accurately, a feeling too deep for words – to a woman.

What is left to say about the craftsmanship of this passage? Two things: one about what is not said, and one about what is.

If we compare Luke's story to Matthew's, we find a very different picture. Matthew emphasises power – the brooding presence of Herod, the wealth of the Wise Men – and fear: the Slaughter of the Innocents, the flight into Egypt, and the gift of myrrh, all look forward to the crucifixion. It is the dark side of the Nativity: in Luke we see only the sunshine.

And finally, when we look at this short piece of writing, a passage without a shred of historical evidence to support it, we find an image that sums up everything we could desire for a grown-up reading of the Bible. The children can have Baby Jesus, the ox and the ass, the shepherds, the manger – all

the endearing paraphernalia of the school Nativity play. But
for adults Luke gives us a vision of a new kind of greatness:
a woman of equal stature to her husband, a god who comes
in peace, a king who stoops to conquer, a Saviour who cares
for animals as well as humans. Not bad for nineteen verses!

3: Peter follows Jesus to the palace of the high priest (Mark 14: 53–4, 66–72)

Our final passage concerns Peter's denial. The outline of the
story is similar in all four Gospels but the version chosen here
is from Mark. The episode follows on from the Last Supper,
at which Jesus reveals that one of his disciples will betray him
and all his followers will be scattered. Peter asserts in his characteristically robust style that he will stay with Jesus come what
may: Jesus replies that before the cock crows twice, Peter will
have denied him three times. Later that evening Jesus and the
disciples go to Gethsemane and Jesus takes aside Peter, James,
and John. He is in great turmoil and walks away by himself
to beg that he should not be forced to go through with the
crucifixion that awaits him. Twice he returns to find Peter and
his fellows asleep. Suddenly the arrest party is upon him and
after a brief resistance the disciples flee. Jesus is taken away to
the palace of the high priest for trial.

But one disciple does not desert him.

53. And they led Jesus away to the high priest: and with
him were assembled all the chief priests and the elders and
scribes.

54. And Peter followed him afar off, even into the palace of the high priest: and he sat with the servants, and warmed himself at the fire.

[...]

66. And as Peter was beneath in the palace, there cometh one of the maids of the high priest:

67. And when she saw Peter warming himself, she looked upon him, and said, And thou also wast with Jesus of Nazareth.

68. But he denied, saying, I know not, neither understand I what thou sayest. And he went out into the porch; and the cock crew.

69. And a maid saw him again, and began to say to them that stood by, This is one of them.

70. And he denied it again. And a little after, they that stood by said again to Peter, Surely thou art one of them: for thou art a Galilean, and thy speech agreeth thereto.

71. But he began to curse and to swear, saying, I know not this man of whom you speak.

72. And the second time the cock crew. And Peter called to mind the word that Jesus said to him, Before the cock crow twice, thou shalt deny me thrice. And when he thought thereon, he wept.

(Mark 14: 53–4, 66–72)

Despite its brevity, this passage illustrates some very important points. The first is about the treatment of character in the New Testament. So much of the Gospels is about meaning and about narrative. But in the treatment of Peter we find a striking focus on character, on the distinctiveness of the individual man. From the moment we meet him Peter is presented as forthright and impetuous: he follows his Lord without a backward glance, he answers his questions and challenges spontaneously and without reflection, and it is typical of him to be the one who risks his life by following his Saviour into the very stronghold of the enemy. Moreover this boldness continues on to the discovery of the empty tomb, where Peter arrives second but enters first, and to Acts, where it is Peter who first leaps to his feet and rallies the demoralised disciples. This focus on character – such a feature of imaginative literature – is unique in the New Testament. No other figure is treated in quite this way.

But it is not just his character that is striking about Peter. It is his fallibility. He is constantly making a fool of himself by rushing in where angels – sometimes almost literally – fear to tread. He is the one who identifies Jesus as 'the Christ', and is then sternly rebuked for it. He is the one who suggests making a tabernacle for the three semi-divine figures at the Transfiguration: Mark hints that Peter wanted to say something, but wasn't quite sure what. And when Jesus walks on water, Peter decides he'll have a go too, only to find (Matthew 14:28–31; see also John 13:24) that it is not as easy as it seems. This hero of the Gospels and the first part of Acts comes complete with a very recognisable and human identity: the three-dimensional quality that literature enables us to see in our fellow humans.

Fallibility is not a quality that we associate with Jesus. Yet it can scarcely be accidental that in the same chapter that tells of Peter's struggles, Mark depicts Jesus as locked in battle with his destiny and almost cracking under the strain.

Why does all this matter? Because this passage breaks completely new ground. It would have been impossible for the Classical Latin authors of Mark's time for a very simple reason. Classical literature observed a strict division of styles. The high style dealt with the affairs of the great, and allowed serious and even tragic treatment of character. The low style dealt with the affairs of the lower classes – and confined itself to comedy. Neither high nor low style concerned itself with the development and transformation of character: with the highs and lows, the triumphs and tragedies, the successes and failures that constitute everyday life and raise it to the level of greatness.

The episode above is exactly this: everyday life handled with depth and seriousness. Almost all the interactions in the Gospels feature Jesus: Jesus and the disciples, Jesus and the Pharisees, Jesus and the randomly chosen men and women that he meets and makes into vehicles and vessels for his teaching. But here Jesus is otherwise engaged – like Peter, though in a different way, he is on trial – and it is Peter who briefly takes centre stage.

As Erich Auerbach suggests, 'A scene like Peter's denial fits into no antique genre. It is too serious for comedy, too contemporary and everyday for tragedy, politically too insignificant for history – and the form which was given it is one of such immediacy that its like does not exist in the literature of antiquity'.[53] I make no comment on whether or not it happened – whether it is *real*. But it is entirely *realistic*; it could be out of *EastEnders* or *The Archers*. Peter, chilled with shock and dismay, goes to warm himself by the fire, sitting – as a countryman, where else would he sit? – with the servants of the high priest. A serving maid recognises him; he hastily denies any knowledge of Jesus; another repeats the charge, and this time Peter's distinctive Galilean accent betrays him; he blusters and curses; and suddenly, just as his master had foretold, the cock crows again, and the truth bursts upon him.

The turmoil in Peter's soul (one critic invents the term 'pendulation' to express the extremity of the swings between excitement and despair) perhaps prepares him for his leadership role in Acts. Certainly it connects him as a character to troubled figures from the Old Testament – David rebuked by Nathan, Saul in his madness, Job in the darkness scraping his boils with a potsherd, Jonah in the belly of the whale. These are all characters who change and develop; who have hidden depths; who swing from hero to zero; who are transformed by the experiences they undergo.

In Classical Greek literature only the great (Oedipus, Orestes, Medea) could be treated in this way. In the Roman authors of the period even the great did not endure such 'pendulations'. In later periods the technique of realism, with its long gestation through the early modern period and its flowering in the 19th and 20th centuries, made it possible to treat ordinary lives with seriousness and depth: Joe Keller in

All My Sons, Willy Loman (the clue is in the name) in *Death of a Salesman*, are as humble in their backgrounds as some of the disciples, yet they become the arena where great personal and social struggles are played out. This could never have happened without the groundbreaking novelty of the way the Gospel writers constructed their stories: 'It was the story of Christ, with its ruthless mixture of everyday reality with the highest and most sublime tragedy, which had conquered the classical rule of styles.'[54]

3. The sum of the parts: reading the Bible as a unity[55]

The three extracts above show, I hope, that the tools of literary criticism can fruitfully be used to increase our appreciation of the qualities of the Bible. But there is a risk that this will end in a kind of cherry-picking, seeing passages in isolation, and selecting only those passages that we find of merit. Images and phrases from the Bible – 'a house built on sand', 'a still small voice', 'tablets of stone', 'risen from the dead', 'the grapes of wrath' – resonate with us, and even single words ('exodus', 'resurrection', 'revelation') come with a rich freight of associations. But it is not just these fragments, these cherries, that exercise an influence.

The Bible remains stubbornly present in the centre of our literary and imaginative experience, just as churches and cathedrals are unmistakable features of the skyline of our cities, towns and villages. It is easy enough to understand this in the case of musicians and painters. Painters use images and musicians use sound, but their art makes no direct statements about reality: to depict a Madonna and Child, carve a Nativity, or write the music for a Christmas oratorio does not require belief in the virgin birth. But what of writers? Dante, Milton, and Eliot wrote from within the charmed circle of faith, but what of Byron? Shelley? Pound? Yeats? Kafka? Bulgakov? D.H. Lawrence? Steinbeck? Gide? Camus? Henry Miller? Robert Heinlein? Philip Larkin? What was it in the Bible that so stimulated the imagination of these writers, none of whom in any meaningful sense could be called Christian? Why is it that Negro spirituals, for example, call on Moses to free them – even though the slaves in the cotton fields had never been anywhere near Egypt? Why do The Byrds and Bob Dylan draw so heavily on Old Testament texts and imagery? Why does a rock band call itself 'Genesis'?

We mentioned churches above. Just as any guidebook will invite us to see the humblest parish church, not just as a collection of windows and carvings, but as an architectural whole – just as we experience in a great public building, whether sacred or secular, a sense of overall design and unity – so we must seek out the overall architecture and shape of the Bible if we are to truly see it. To do otherwise is not only bad literary criticism, but bad Bible criticism.

The first principle of the appreciation of any work of art is that it is a unity. That unity may not be obvious at first sight: but that is the principle that must guide us. The two Appendices show how much editing and rewriting the Bible has undergone, making it 'probably the most systematically constructed sacred book in the world'.[56] In Parts One and Two I used this to argue against claims for any kind of historical truth for the Old and New Testaments. But if we view the work from the perspective of the imagination, we are reminded that editing can be object-ive, a process designed, not to impose order and unity, but to find it. The good editor can sometimes see what the author cannot, just as the artist can find in the landscape an order that nature has not put there, and the historian, a pattern in events undetectable to those who took part. Editing is a process that works in many ways and on many levels. There is grouping by genre; just as Shakespeare's works were divided by his first publishers into histories, tragedies, and comedies, so the books of the Old Testament are grouped into Pentateuch, Histories, Prophets, and 'others'. There is editing by combination, as when the Redactor interweaves the two tales of Noah's flood into a single apparently unified story. And there is thematic editing and grouping: the Book of Isaiah, despite its title, cannot have a unity of authorship unless Isaiah lived for over 300 years, but it has nonetheless a unity of theme, 'the parable of Israel lost, captive, and redeemed'.[57]

The picture 'Saint Luke painting the Virgin and Child', a 15th-century miniature from the British Library collection, is instructive in this regard. Saint Luke sits before the Virgin and paints her: but what appears on the canvas is not quite what sits before him. On his canvas, the Virgin's red hair is largely covered: the child's pose is more tranquil, less teasing; the mood is more contemplative and reverent than that of the sitters who face him. The painting shows Luke editing what he sees before him to bring out its true but hidden meaning.

We see this editing perhaps most clearly where it has been left incomplete. The opening of John's Gospel – 'In the beginning …' – was unmistakably written in order that the New Testament should open with a creation story to match the creation story that opens Genesis. Alas, John's Gospel was not only written later than the others (which wouldn't matter given that Matthew was later than Mark, but is placed before it), but was for many years regarded as of questionable value and orthodoxy, so it never took the pole position for which it was intended.

So we see everywhere evidence of deliberate design and redesign both within and between the Testaments. Anton Ehrenzweig wrote of 'the hidden order of art'. What is the hidden order that editors detected in the Bible? Rather than trying to view the parts, let us try to look at the whole, and just as we give credit to a church or a cathedral as having a unity of design, let us make the hypothesis that the editors of the Bible too were striving to find and give voice to the unity, the hidden order, lying within its apparent shapelessness. Let us approach it as we approach any work of the imagination – as a unity.

The unity of Old and New Testament: myth …
We cannot begin to make sense of the New Testament, and thereby of the unity of the Bible as a whole, without appreciating the overwhelming importance that the evangelists attached to showing how Jesus fulfils what was 'foretold in the Scriptures' – by which of course they meant the Old Testament.

The first term we need in order to understand imaginative works is that of myth (from the Greek 'mythos', meaning story). For all its historical content, the Bible is not a work of history; much of what it contains did happen, and therefore features also in works of history, but it is not in the Bible for that reason. Myth, as we will define it here, has two elements. One is imagination – a quality that myth shares with all other forms of fictional writing. But myths have another dimension. They tackle matters that society deems to be important: they cluster around areas of social or existential concern, and the greater the concern – the closer to the central beliefs, and anxieties, of that society – the more they tend to hang together and form that set of interlocking tales that we call a mythology. Classical mythology, which underpinned Homer and Sophocles, clustered round Zeus and the Olympians: it was 'canonical' – sacred – to the Greeks. For a Christian audience, it became 'merely' mythology. Our own canonical myth is the Bible.

Myth is not history, and mythical thinking – though highly structured – is not rational and analytical thinking. History looks outwards and is judged by its correspondence with external reality. Myth looks inwards and has a different standard of truth: its fidelity is to shape, structure, and meaning. Shakespeare read his historical sources carefully and used them well, but *Hamlet* and *Macbeth* are structured as tragedies, myths about kingship. Gibbon's *Decline and Fall* is a work of history: but the pattern of rise and fall alluded to in its title – of the tragic hero, of the sun, and ultimately of a sun god – is a mythic one, and retains its literary and imaginative power long after Gibbon's work has been superseded as history.

History seldom repeats itself: myth always does, because matters of social and existential concern, like the rituals that reflect them, need to be constantly revisited and renewed. Structure – shape, pattern, and above all repetition – is present everywhere in the Old Testament. The most striking example of this is the parallelism between Old and New Testament. Augustine remarked that the Old and New Testaments are a kind of sealed unit, like a pair of mirrors reflecting each other, so that the New Testament lies hidden in the Old, and the Old Testament is revealed in the New. We have examined at length the way in which such correspondence undermines any historical claims made for the Bible. But by the same token, such correspondence only reinforces its integrity and power as myth. When early Christians looked for reassurance about Jesus they were told to go to 'the Scriptures' – which meant at that time, not the New Testament, but the Old. (When in 140 AD Marcion suggested a canon without the Old Testament, he was excommunicated.) We have seen the tremendous efforts made by the evangelists and the writers of the Epistles to create their own Old Testament 'prequels'. Historically speaking there was no evidence to find: but mythical evidence is of a different kind.

The myth of deliverance: synchronising Old and New Testaments

The core myth of the Bible is the myth of deliverance: the U-shaped fall and rise of descent and recovery. Let us examine this by picking out seven such narrative structures in the work (there are more, but these will do!).

	1	2	3	4	5	6	7	or 7
	Garden of Eden	Promised Land 1 (Abraham)	Promised Land 2 (Moses, Joshua)	Jerusalem, Zion (David, Solomon)	Return and rebuilt Temple	Purified Temple	Jesus' spiritual kingdom	Messiah of Judaism
	Genesis	Genesis	Exodus, Joshua	Samuel, Kings	Ezra, Nehemiah	Maccabees	New Testament	
	Exile, Cities of the Plain	Egypt, Red Sea, Wilderness	Philistines, Canaanites etc.	Babylon, Nebuchadnezzar	Antiochus Epiphanes abomination	Rome, Nero		

Diagram 9. Fall and redemption (adapted from H. Northrop Frye, The Great Code: the Bible and Literature (Houghton Mifflin Harcourt, 1981), used by permission of Victoria University in the University of Toronto).

In each case the top line – the starting point – represents the unfallen world, the natural home of man, the good life lived in harmony with the teaching of God. The bottom line represents the fallen world of exile from that ideal state. In each case there is a 'deliverance' from the fallen state up to the recovered good life, and in each case – as we move left to right – there is a new fall from grace. (The line splits at the right-hand end according to whether Jesus is seen from a Jewish or a Christian perspective.) Each of these events is a myth, whether or not it is a historical event: the historical pattern is at best doubtful, but the structural, that is mythical, shape is impossible to miss.

If the core myth of the Bible is deliverance, then the core myth of deliverance is Exodus, and if we are to understand why the writers of the New Testament draw so heavily on the Old, this is where we need to start. So many puzzles in the Gospels become clear when we understand the urgent wish of the evangelists to conform the life of Jesus to the patterns of the Old Testament. The child Jesus *descends* into Egypt with his parents, and (in John's Gospel) *descends* into human form, just as the Israelites *descend* into captivity in Egypt. The Passion is synchronised with the Passover, calling to mind the Passover deliverance of the Israelites. The sacrifice of the firstborn in Exodus is echoed not only in Matthew's Slaughter of the Innocents, but in the crucifixion itself. At the Passover, the firstborn is replaced by a lamb, giving rise to the identification of Jesus as 'the lamb of God'. Before the crucifixion comes the curious episode when the mob choose Barabbas over Jesus, a 'tradition' without any precedent in Roman or Jewish custom: this becomes much easier to understand in terms of a kind of 'younger brother' (Barabbas means 'son of the father', in other words 'brother', in Aramaic), reminding us of the recurring theme of fraternal rivalry and supplanting of the firstborn (Cain/Abel, Ishmael/Isaac, Esau/Jacob) running through the Old Testament.*

The Christian ritual of baptism, submerging the believer so that they can emerge into new life and leave their sins behind, echoes the Israelite crossing of the Red Sea and their escape from captivity into freedom.

While in the wilderness the Israelites are troubled by serpents and ask Moses for help; he raises a healing serpent on a staff (Numbers 21:9), prefiguring the elevation of Jesus on a cross as the healer of his people. How long does Moses spend on Mount Sinai writing down the words of the Lord? Forty days. How long does Jesus spend in the wilderness on his way to save the world? Forty days. How many tribes leave Israel? Twelve. How many disciples does Jesus appoint? ...

---

* In Leviticus 14:4–7 and 49–53, we find the same pattern: to heal the community from leprosy, the priest takes two birds, kills one, and releases the other after dipping it in the blood. We remember the crowds in Matthew 27:25 crying, 'His blood be on us ...'.

There are many more examples but it would be tedious to cite them all.*

The point is that for the New Testament writers and their readers, the events of the life of Jesus had no meaning unless and until they corresponded with a prefiguring event in the Old Testament. This approach to Scripture is known to scholars medieval and modern as 'typological' or 'figural', and it explains why for a century or more after the death of Jesus, the 'Scripture' to which believers were referred for illumination about the life of Christ was not the evolving New Testament, but the pre-existent Old Testament, written before Jesus was

---

* We might also point out the parallelism in birth between Moses, the Old Testament hero, and Jesus, the hero of the New Testament: Jesus is placed in a manger and provided with a kind of dual parentage – God and Joseph – reflecting the way that Moses is placed in an ark of bulrushes, and brought up both by his humble birth mother and by the daughter of Pharaoh (Exodus Chapter 2). The Old Testament Law is given on Mount Sinai; it is not an accident that the sermon giving the new law, the revised contract between God and man, is also given on a mount. The repeated food miracles in the New Testament, feeding Israelites in the wilderness with loaves and fishes, reflect the miraculous feeding of the Israelites with manna in Exodus; Jesus' death, descent, and resurrection echo respectively the Angel of Death at the Passover in Egypt, the Israelites' crossing of the Red Sea, and their escape into freedom. Moses dies on the verge of the Promised Land and it is Joshua who brings the exiles home to their inheritance: in the same way, according to the New Testament writers, the Law of Moses fails on the edge of salvation, and it is left to the child Jesus (Jesus and Joshua are the same name) to establish the New Testament and accomplish the task.

even born. Beneath this 'figural' approach lies a belief in the deeper meaning of events, rather than the surface: 'The Gospel writers care nothing about the kind of evidence that would interest a biographer – remarks of disinterested travellers and the like; they care only about comparing the events in their accounts of Jesus with what the Old Testament, as they read it, said would happen to the messiah ... [Their view is that] This may not be what you would have seen if you had been there, but what you would have seen would have missed the whole point of what was really going on.'[58]

Metaphorical thinking

Mythical thinking is also metaphorical thinking. A metaphor is something that stands for something else: Egypt stands for captivity, the lamb for Jesus, the cross for salvation, the city of Jerusalem for the Heavenly City. In the diagram above, each item on the top line is a metaphor or 'type' for the ideal condition of man, his true home, and each item on the bottom line for the fallen state of man, his life in exile and captivity. As such, all the high points are metaphorically identical with each other, and likewise all the low points. 'The garden of Eden, the Promised Land, Jerusalem, and Mount Zion are interchangeable synonyms for the home of the soul, and in Christian imagery they are all identical.'[59] And what they are identical with, for New Testament writers, is the Kingdom of God that Jesus spoke of. (From a Jewish perspective, the Hebrew Bible points likewise to the redeemed world that the Jewish messiah will usher in.) The same is true along the bottom line, where Wilderness and Egypt, Babylon and Rome, are metaphors for each other, and hence, in mythical thought, identical and interchangeable. And the deliverers of Israel along the top line are all 'types' of the final deliverer, whether Christian Saviour or Jewish messiah.

In the top line, God, man, and nature are in harmony. The close contact between man and God scarcely needs emphasising, but man stands between a spiritual realm and a natural one, and the relationship with nature takes different forms in the two domains. In the lower world, the relationship between man and nature is one of domination. In this alienated world the task of humans is merely to 'Be fruitful, and multiply, and replenish the earth and subdue it, and have dominion over … every living thing that moveth upon the earth' (Genesis 1:28). This world of exile and wandering, of thorns and thistles, of human and animal enslavement ('And the fear of you and the dread of you shall be upon every beast of the earth', Genesis 9:2), is the fallen world of Egypt and Babylon, of tyranny between husband and wife (Genesis 3:16), and of Ezekiel's valley of dry bones, into which Jesus traditionally descends after his crucifixion. It is also the totalitarian hell of a world of pointless work designed only to subjugate nature and accumulate wealth: 'For what shall it profit a man, if he shall gain the whole world, and lose his own soul?' (Mark 8:36).

Its counterpart in the higher world is the Garden of Eden, where man names the animals as if they were pets, and lives in gentle harmony with the trees and plants. That harmony with nature recurs in the Promised Land, which will be 'flowing with milk and honey', in Isaiah's holy mountain where 'the wolf also shall dwell with the lamb' and 'they shall not hurt nor destroy' (Isaiah 11:6–9), and in the Book of Revelation, where the river of the water of life will flow through the City of God, and the tree of life will produce its healing fruit (Revelation 22:1–2). The purpose of work in the Bible is to regain that higher world: 'And when you work with love you bind yourself to yourself, and to one another, and to God … work is love made visible' (Kahlil Gibran).

Abraham brings his family up out of Ur to a promised land in the West; Moses and Joshua bring the Israelites up out of Egypt and return them to the Promised Land; both are 'types' of deliverance. But the New Testament writers need to combine other 'types' of authority into the figure of Jesus, notably those of prophet and (given that Israel is a theocracy) king. As king, he is the descendant of David, born in Bethlehem into a humble family; and the evangelists take pains to connect him also to Solomon, builder of the Temple, through the homage of the Wise Men from the East whose gifts echo those brought by the Queen of Sheba ('And the Gentiles shall come to thy light, and kings to the brightness of thy rising … all they from Sheba shall come: they shall bring gold and incense: and they shall shew forth the praises of the LORD', Isaiah 60:3–6). As prophet, Jesus fulfils the 'types' of Moses (the representative of the Law) and of Elijah, the greatest prophet of the Old Testament but also a 'type' of Jesus in his concern for the poor and his ability to raise the dead (1 Kings 17–24): both appear in the otherwise rather mysterious Transfiguration that features in all three Synoptics (Matthew 17:1–9, Mark 9:2–8, Luke 9:28–36). Nothing in the New Testament is there for itself: everything is there to fulfil the Old.

Religion and control

Followers of the three main Western religions – Judaism, Christianity, and Islam – are collectively known as 'people of the book', and all three 'books' function as rulebooks and instruction manuals for religious and moral orthodoxy. It is commonplace to hear people speak of 'Judaeo-Christian morality' and I suspect I have even used the phrase in this book. The sense of the Bible as a book of rules was always there, but – as we have seen – has become more pressing with the rise of Protestant religions (and their Islamic equivalents) which accept no authority other than their own direct and context-free reading of Scripture.

Religion (from the Latin root 'binding') is always concerned to demarcate and exclude – believers from non-believers, orthodox from heretics, the saved from the damned, saints from sinners, good from evil, clean from polluted, the sacred from the secular. In like manner, faith is always under pressure to close itself off from doubt. Professed faith is a statement of loyalty – to belief, to practice, and to fellow-believers – and like the soldier preparing for battle, believers must shut out any questioning of their own rightness (and righteousness). Faith strikes a bargain with God, and expects that the bargain will be fulfilled: 'Honour thy father and thy mother: *that thy days may be long upon the land which the Lord thy God giveth thee*' (Exodus 20:12, italics added). And all religions are communities of practice, of rules of behaviour and conduct that members must follow if they are to stay within the community.

Where there are rules, there are enforcers of the rules. All who create and enforce rules – all regulators – must speak with authority, and the Bible is no exception. Indeed it is not an accident that we use the word 'speak'. The authority of rules is deeply associated for us with speech: military words of command, the Queen's (or the King's) Speech, the word of the Lord dictated to Moses, the commandments dictated in turn by Moses to the assembled Hebrews. And the sentence structures and rhythms of such speech are very oral ones, using short sentences with a distinctive, often repetitive rhythm and an absolute confidence and clarity that excludes nuance, explanation, or qualification:

'Ye have heard that it was said by them of old time, Thou shalt not commit adultery: But I say unto you, That whosoever looketh on a woman to lust after her hath committed adultery with her already in his heart. And if thy right eye offend thee, pluck it out, and cast it from thee: for it is profitable for thee that one of thy members should perish, and not that thy whole body should be cast into hell. And if thy right hand offend thee, cut it off, and cast it from thee: for it is profitable for thee that one of thy members should perish, and not that thy whole body should be cast into hell.' (Matthew 5:27–30)

The Sermon on the Mount – for which the 'type' is the Ten Commandments, also delivered on a mount – speaks the simple language of vision and prophecy. But rules are always more complex in the application than in the announcing, and require in practice much interpretation, qualification, and glossing.

The process of clarifying, interpreting, and qualifying, of turning the inspiration of prophecy into the rules and regulations of religion, is the work of scribes. The writings that interpret the Torah (the midrash) are longer than the Torah itself, and the hadith and tafsir likewise longer than the Qur'an. The Gospels remind us that Jesus spoke often, but wrote only once, and it is not accidental that he wrote in sand (John 8:6–8), emphasising the paradox that the spoken word can sometimes last longer than the written. What scribes do is scribble. What prophets do is prophesy.

But it is not only law-givers (and dictators) who speak with authority. So do oracles. And if we reframe this authoritative voice, not as the dictatorial voice of the law-giver, but as the oracular and inspired voice of the prophet and seer, we get a very different perspective on what is being said. What if, instead of rules, the prophets are giving us a vision? What if, instead of the written and codified tyranny of organised religion – the written script of how things should be – we are hearing instead the inspired and authentic spoken voice of how things might be: a vision of a world without killing or deception, of a society without tyranny or injustice?

Read this way, the Bible becomes a very different book: different not because the words are different, but because the purpose, the meaning, and the context of the words have changed. Visions, like compass bearings, are directions, not destinations: there, not to arrive at, but to steer by. Isaiah's holy mountain cannot be found on any map, nor is it surrounded by signs forbidding killing. '[In this reading], "Thou shalt not kill" … is less important as a law than as a vision of an ideal world in which people do not, perhaps even cannot, kill … many of Jesus' exhortations … are not guides to practice … but parts of a vision of an "innocent" world, and it is that vision which is the guide to practice.'*[60]

We know about vision, oddly enough, because we respond to it in the inspirational speeches of politics. 'We shall fight on the beaches, we shall fight on the landing grounds, we shall fight in the fields and in the streets, we shall fight in the hills; we shall never surrender', is not a battle plan. 'A rainbow nation' is not a statement about demographics. 'Government of the people, by the people,

---

* The commandments about killing and adultery, for example, are not the absolute prohibitions that they may seem. The prohibition on killing did not apply to war, to capital punishment, or to non-Israelites, as the Old Testament abundantly demonstrates. And the prohibition on adultery does not apply to men. It is aimed at the sexual conduct of a married or betrothed woman, the point being, not the preservation of chastity, but the protection of the husband's lineage against the risk that he might raise a child not his own, a cuckoo in his nest.

and for the people', is not a worked-through constitutional proposal, and 'I have a dream' is not a White Paper on racial integration. They are all phrased – both in their syntax and in their impact – as prophecies; as authoritative statements of how things could be; as visions.

When in the Sermon on the Mount (Matthew 5:32) we read, 'Whosoever shall put away his wife [...] causeth her to commit adultery', we recognise the authentic voice of prophecy. But where the brackets are, someone has inserted a qualifier, 'saving for the cause of fornication'. As Northrop Frye memorably puts it, 'Some scholars think that [that] phrase ... is a later interpolation. One reason why they think so is stylistic: the cautious legal cough of parenthesis has no place in a prophetic style, but is a sign that someone is try-ing to corrupt the gospel into a new law.'[61] The voice of prophecy is the roar of the lion, not the officious chatter of the squirrel. Corrupting a Gospel into a law is a recipe for tyranny, a choice, in the words of Deuteronomy (30:19), of death over life.

The Bible and dissent

Where religion seeks to control, vision seeks to liberate. The imagination, which is where vision resides, is always in opposition because its limits are not the permissible, but the conceivable. The real-world settings of so much of the Bible, its profound if problematic immersion in history, together with its concern for the underdog, mean that its vision will always challenge the rich and the powerful. The Torah enjoins charity to widows and orphans, and reminds the people of Israel that even when they are installed in their Promised Land, 'Love ye therefore the stranger: for ye were strangers in the land of Egypt' (Deuteronomy 10:19). Jesus remarks on the widow who drops her mite in the Temple collection box (Mark 12:41–44, Luke 21:1–4) and in doing so, condemns the rich and powerful who could give so much more.

This profound feeling for justice marks a huge area of common ground between the Bible and literature. Myths are where the poetic imagination meets social concern: and that is where artists, writers, and poets work. When John Steinbeck was outraged by the treatment of itinerant farm workers in the Midwest, he kept much of the content of his novel as close to realism as he could, and indeed the story (and the history) are shocking and distressing enough to need no embroidery. But by choosing to call his book *The Grapes of Wrath*, he connected the pathos of humble Okie sharecroppers to a greater story. The grapes of wrath feature in Julia Ward Howes' 'Battle Hymn of the Republic' from 1861, linking these ordinary men and women with the mighty struggle to free the slaves and beyond that with the sacrifice made by Christ ('As Christ died to make men holy, let us die to make them free'); and that in its turn points to 'the great winepress of the wrath of God' (Revelation 14:19–20) and the conviction that what awakes the anger of God is above all injustice. And behind the realism of content in Steinbeck's book is a further mythical structure equally charged with echoes and resonances. The journey to California becomes a failed Exodus, the name of

A VISION OF FREEDOM

the heroine (Rose of Sharon) points us to the Song of Songs, and the extraordinary ending where she feeds the starving old man with her own milk echoes Lot's daughters baring their young bodies to their ageing father. The preacher Jim Casy (the initials are a pointer) loses his faith and turns away from his former life: but by his death seeking to 'speak truth to power', he becomes a figure of Christ.

'And it came to pass, when Ahab saw Elijah, that Ahab said to him, "Art thou he that troubleth Israel?"' (1 Kings 18:17). The priestly establishment supports kingship (and indeed eventually turns into the theocracy of Jesus' time), but Elijah was a prophet, and the prophets of the Old Testament are a notoriously rebellious bunch, well known for their habit of speaking truth to power – whatever the cost to themselves. Moses, and before him Abraham, bargain and negotiate with God; Nathan confronts David; Elijah confronts Ahab; in the New Testament, John the Baptist pays with his head for the threat he represents to Herod. And there is in the Old Testament a general uneasiness about power, a sense that if not now, then soon, it will end in tears. Samuel, following the advice of God, warns the Israelites against appointing a king to rule them (1 Samuel 8); they choose not to take his advice but it is soon proved to have been correct. The Deuteronomist, similarly sceptical about the whole business of kingship (Deuteronomy 17:15–20), observes the actions of the successive kings of Israel with disapproval, consistently marking them down for their failure to centralise sacrifice in Jerusalem and keep to the strict letter

THE SUM OF THE PARTS

of the Law: kingship, he seems to suggest, may be necessary, but it is a necessary evil.*

When the priest Hilkiah finds the celebrated scroll of the Torah in Deuteronomy in 622 BC and arranges for it to be read to the young King Josiah, it is the king who weeps and rends his garments: and what is more, it is the king, not the priest, who insists that it must be brought to the knowledge of the people, the work of being the chosen ones of God being for all the people, not just the priests.

As we might expect, the revolutionary forces in the Old Testament become focused in the condensing mirror of the New, where even in the Temple itself God is praised as the one who 'hath put down the mighty from their seats' (Luke 1:52). Jesus' constant campaigns against the Temple establishment are well known, as is his insistence that the disciples are never to join the cosy group of those who conform: 'Woe unto you, when all men shall speak well of you!' (Luke 6:26). His statements that he comes not to bring peace but a sword are played down by evangelists and St Paul alike; but we notice that although Paul enjoins Christians to accept and obey the laws of the land, he does not want them to set their moral compass by those laws. As in the Old Testament, what you

---

* The Geneva Bible of 1560, product of a radical Protestantism, frequently glosses 'king' as 'tyrant'. The more cautious Authorised Version of 1611, commissioned and approved by King James, never once uses this term (Alister McGrath, *In the Beginning: The Story of the King James Bible,* 2001, p. 143).

find in 'high places' is 'spiritual wickedness' (Ephesians 6:12). And when we get to Revelation we are left in no doubt: Rome – like Egypt, like Babylon, like the Cities of the Plain – is the seat of Antichrist.

Imagination and vision

Is this a programme for political action, a kind of early Marxism? By no means. Read in this way, the Bible is not revolutionary in the sense that Chairman Mao or Islamic State are revolutionary, blueprints for an earthly kingdom. If it was, it would be the first work to be banned in such a kingdom. The fate of Socrates in Athens, of poets in Plato's Republic, of visionaries in Augustine's City of God, and (of course) of Jesus in Jerusalem, shows that there is no room for the unfettered imagination in the Heavenly City, because its limits always go beyond what is, towards what might be: beyond what is prescribed, towards what is possible; beyond what is allowed, towards what can be imagined.

When we set aside theology and history, we find ourselves looking at the Bible as a structure of the imagination, and viewing it through the lens of the imagination. It is striking that all serious religions have a close and continuing association with the human products of culture that we call art: the statues and stupas of Buddhism, the mosques and minarets of Islam, the cathedrals and the church music of Christianity, the poetry of the Psalms. E.M. Forster rightly remarks in *Aspects of the Novel* that 'great art is like great religion: it forces you out into the world on its service': the community of the imagination is not a closed community of belief but an open community of vision. When Donne proclaims that 'no man is an island, entire of itself ... any man's death diminishes me', the truth of the statement is immaterial. It is a call to live, and to act, as if it was true.

When we read it in this way, the world imagined in the Bible is not so much discovered as rediscovered. Wordsworth's instinct that 'The Soul that rises with us, our life's Star/Hath had elsewhere its setting,/And cometh from afar', and his glimpse of 'the vision splendid' that attends the youth but 'fades into the light of common day'; Baudelaire's 'Les vrais paradis sont les paradis qu'on a perdus' and 'Le génie, c'est l'enfance retrouvée'* – these spring from the same sense of a world that we come from – and long to return to. The core myth of the Bible is deliverance, and its core metaphors are the city and the garden: deliverance is not just deliverance from, but deliverance to, and it is to the transformed and renewed Garden of Eden and City of God, symbols of our true home, that the Bible longs to return, to 'arrive where we started' and 'know the place for the first time'.

Just as place is rediscovered, so is time. When after long wandering in the wilderness the weary reader reaches *Le Temps Retrouvé* (*Time Rediscovered*), the final volume of Proust's mighty work, he finds that along with the promised rediscovery of time there is a rediscovery of self and of human

---

★ 'The real paradises are the paradises one has lost'; 'Genius is childhood rediscovered'.

grandeur: we realise that the quirky and fallible characters of his story are 'giants in time', and that the time in which they are giants is the timeless world of eternity, time rediscovered and reinterpreted, not the endlessly repeated time of the fallen world. And just as time and place are revealed in this imagined world, so too is our acquaintance with a different vision of God: not Blake's 'Accuser who is the God of this world', but the 'abba' that Jesus speaks to, the God who learns, who changes his mind, who allows himself to be persuaded (Genesis 2:19, 8:21, 18), who gently and ironically celebrates his own inconsistency (Jonah 4:11), and who watches over the fall of a sparrow (Matthew 10:29). This is not a world of an inflexible and intimidating perfection, but one in which we can say with Wallace Stevens that 'the imperfect [the unfinished, the not-yet-complete] is our Paradise'.

Milton saw the Bible with its recurring upward movement as 'a manifesto of human freedom'.[62] What gets in the way of freedom, and appears when seen through a theological filter as sin, becomes in the language of the visionary imagination a fear of freedom, the feeling that Sartre characterised as an effort to flee from the 'pour soi' to the 'en soi',* to pretend that we are the prisoners of our past rather than the makers

---

* A thing or an animal is 'en soi' ('in itself'), without free will. A human, in Sartre's view, is 'pour soi' ('for itself'), having no fixed identity, and so having to choose who to be. Sartre saw people as trying to get rid of this frightening freedom by pretending to have a fixed personality (a soldier, a waiter, an anti-Semite), in other words to be 'en soi' rather than 'pour soi'.

of our own future. Freedom that restores to us our own creative powers, that reminds us that we have created the gods to which we bow down, is hard work and requires discipline and a readiness to accept the responsibility that it brings for our own actions and their consequences. The Bible has been made into an instrument of divine tyranny, but like all great powers of culture, it is a work of the human imagination, and artists have always recognised that. Properly understood it celebrates our recapture of our own imaginings. Its message is the appeal of Tennyson's ageing but vigorous Ulysses to his faithful crew: 'Come, my friends/'Tis not too late to seek a newer world ...'

APPENDIX 1:
BOOKS OF THE OLD TESTAMENT

This list represents my best guess but would certainly not find agreement among scholars on all points. It may seem confusing. This is because it is. Every book of the Bible has been rewritten, edited, and generally mashed up, before reaching its present form; just look at the Book of Isaiah, which spreads over three centuries. But more than this, every book of the Bible has then been repositioned, rather as one shuffles and deals a pack of cards, to give it the place in the canon that the Old Testament editors felt was right for it. Consider Micah, one of the earliest books but positioned at number 33 in the final sequence. All this was done in the period between about 928 BC (the split into the northern kingdom of Israel and the southern kingdom of Judah), and about 200 BC, when the texts began to achieve a final version with the production of the Greek Septuagint.

Everything is further confused by the technique of 'pseudepigraphy', whereby later authors write works under the name of an earlier author. This is particularly useful when they want to create a prophecy that a later event has fulfilled ('postdiction'). Daniel (see 4th and 2nd centuries below) was particularly subject to this.

Modern scholarship constantly reviews the data and comes up with new hypotheses: this list will change!

	Books of the Old Testament as placed in Christian Bible (Hebrew Bible differs)	Books of the Old Testament in the order in which they were (probably) first written down. Note that this is much contested.
	The Pentateuch	928–722 BC (the period of the J and E authors)
1.	Genesis	The J and E elements of Genesis, Exodus, Numbers
2.	Exodus	(Some of) Psalms
3.	Leviticus	? (Some of) Song of Solomon
4.	Numbers	
5	Deuteronomy	8th century BC
		Hosea, Amos, Micah
		Isaiah 1–39
		? (Parts of) Proverbs
	The Historical Books	
6.	Joshua	715–687 BC (the Priestly author)
7.	Judges	The Priestly elements of Genesis, Exodus, Leviticus, Numbers
8.	Ruth	
9.	1 Samuel	7th century BC
10.	2 Samuel	Nahum, Habakkuk, Zephaniah
11.	1 Kings	? Job
12.	2 Kings	Jeremiah, the first part of Deuteronomy, and Joshua, Judges, 1 and 2 Samuel, and 1 and 2 Kings

	Books of the Old Testament as placed in Christian Bible (Hebrew Bible differs)	Books of the Old Testament in the order in which they were (probably) first written down. Note that this is much contested.
13.	1 Chronicles	
14.	2 Chronicles	
15.	Ezra	6th century BC (the exile in Babylon)
16.	Nehemiah	The second part of Deuteronomy, and 'in exile' edits of Joshua, Judges, 1 and 2 Samuel, 1 and 2 Kings
17.	Esther	Isaiah 40–55
		(Some of) Psalms
		Lamentations, Ezekiel, Obadiah, Haggai
	The Poetical and Wisdom Books	
18.	Job	
19.	Psalms	
20.	Proverbs	
21.	Ecclesiastes	5th century BC (return from exile, rebuilding Jerusalem): the Redactor
22.	Song of Solomon	Final edit of Genesis, Exodus, Leviticus, Numbers, Deuteronomy, together with Joshua, Judges, 1 and 2 Samuel, 1 and 2 Kings
		Ruth
		Ezra, Nehemiah

	Books of the Old Testament as placed in Christian Bible (Hebrew Bible differs)	Books of the Old Testament in the order in which they were (probably) first written down. Note that this is much contested.
	The Prophetic Books	Proverbs (final edit)
23.	Isaiah	? Song of Solomon (final edit)
24.	Jeremiah	Isaiah 56–66
25.	Lamentations	Zechariah, Malachi
26.	Ezekiel	
27	Daniel	**4th century BC**
28.	Hosea	1 and 2 Chronicles
29.	Joel	Ecclesiastes
30.	Amos	Joel
31.	Obadiah	Daniel 1–6 (the court tales)
32.	Jonah	
33.	Micah	**3rd century BC**
34.	Nahum	Esther
35.	Habakkuk	Jonah
36.	Zephaniah	
37.	Haggai	**2nd century BC**
38.	Zechariah	Daniel 7–12 (the apocalyptic material)
39.	Malachi	

APPENDIX 2:
BOOKS OF THE NEW TESTAMENT

	... in their printed order as finalised in the 4th century AD	... in probable order of (main) composition (much contested!)
		40s AD onwards: Epistles attributed to Paul:
1.	Matthew	1 Thessalonians
2.	Mark	Galatians
3.	Luke	1 Corinthians
4.	John	Philippians
5	Acts of the Apostles	Philemon
6.	Romans	2 Corinthians
7.	1 Corinthians	Romans
8.	2 Corinthians	Colossians (probably)
9.	Galatians	2 Thessalonians (probably)
10.	Ephesians	James (not by Paul)
	Fall of Jerusalem and destruction of the Second Temple in 70 AD	
		70s–90s: Gospels, Revelation, probably Acts:
11.	Philippians	Mark (about 70)
12.	Colossians	Matthew (85–95)
13.	1 Thessalonians	Luke (85–95)
		John (v1 70 AD, v2 95 AD)

	... in their printed order as finalised in the 4th century AD	... in probable order of (main) composition (much contested!)
14.	2 Thessalonians	Acts of the Apostles (may be later)
15.	1 Timothy	Revelation
16.	2 Timothy	
		90–120: non-Pauline Epistles:
17.	Titus	Ephesians
18.	Philemon	Hebrews
19.	Hebrews	Jude
20.	James	1 Peter
21.	1 Peter	1 Timothy
22	2 Peter	2 Timothy
23.	1 John	Titus
24.	2 John	1 John
25.	3 John	2 John
26.	Jude	3 John
27.	Revelation	2 Peter

BIBLIOGRAPHY

Aslan, Reza, 2013, *Zealot: The Life and Times of Jesus of Nazareth*

Auerbach, Erich, 1953, *Mimesis: The Representation of Reality in Western Literature*

Barton, John, 1997, *What is the Bible?* (2nd edition)

Barton, John, 2010, *The Bible: the Basics*

Barton, John, and Muddiman, John, 2001, *The Oxford Bible Commentary*

Beeching, Paul Q., 1997, *Awkward Reverence: Reading the New Testament Today*

Bickerman, E.J., 1986, 'Utilitas Crucis' (1935), reprinted in *Studies in Jewish and Christian History III*

Charlesworth, J.H., 1990, *John and the Dead Sea Scrolls*

Chartres, Caroline (ed.), 2006, *Why I Am Still an Anglican*

Cohn, Norman, 1957, *The Pursuit of the Millennium*

Coogan, Michael D (ed.), 2001, *The New Oxford Annotated Bible*, 4th edition

Cupitt, Don, 1980, *Taking Leave of God*

Dewey, David, 2004, *Which Bible? A Guide to English Translations*

Douglas, Mary, 1966, *Purity and Danger*

Eisenbaum, Pamela, 2009, *Paul Was Not a Christian*

Festinger, Reicken and Schachter, 1964, *When Prophecy Fails*

Foster, Paul, 2009, *The Apocryphal Gospels: A Very Short Introduction*

Fredriksen, Paula, 2000, *From Jesus to Christ (2nd edition)*

Fredriksen, Paula, 2000, *Jesus of Nazareth, King of the Jews*

Friedman, Richard E., 1988, *Who Wrote the Bible?*

Friedman, Richard E., 2003, *The Bible with Sources Revealed*

Frye, H. Northrop, 1957, *The Anatomy of Criticism*

Frye, H. Northrop, 1976, *The Secular Scripture: A Study of the Structure of Romance*

Frye, H. Northrop, 1981, *The Great Code: the Bible and Literature*

Gager, John, 1975, *Kingdom and Community: The Social World of Early Christianity*

Gaston, Lloyd, 1970, *No Stone on Another: Studies in the Significance of the Fall of Jerusalem in the Synoptic Gospels*

Gibran, Kahlil, 1923, *The Prophet*

Harris, Marvin, 1977, 'The Lamb of Mercy', in *Cannibals and Kings: the Origins of Culture*

James, William, 1902, *Varieties of Religious Experience*

Lane Fox, Robin, 1991, *The Unauthorised Version: Truth and Fiction in the Bible*

Leach, Sir Edmund, 1969, 'Genesis as Myth', 'The Legitimacy of Solomon', and 'Virgin Birth', in *Genesis as Myth and Other Essays*

McGrath, Alister, 2001, *In the Beginning: The Story of the King James Bible*

Mack, Burton, 1988, *A Myth of Innocence: Mark and Christian Origins*

Major, H.D.A., 1925, *Jesus by an Eye-Witness*

Morison, Frank, 1930, *Who Moved the Stone?*

Ord and Coote, 1994, *Is the Bible True? Understanding the Bible Today*

Powell, Mark A., 1988, *The Jesus Debate*

Ratzinger, Joseph, 2012, *Jesus of Nazareth: The Infancy Narratives*

Riches, John, 2000, *The Bible: A Very Short Introduction*

Robinson, Ian, 1973, *The Survival of English: Essays in Criticism of Language*

Rubinstein, R.E., 2000, *When Jesus Became God*

Sand, Shlomo, 2009, *The Invention of the Jewish People*

Sanders, E.P., 1985, *Jesus and Judaism*

Schweitzer, Albert, 1906, *The Quest for the Historical Jesus*

Thompson, Thomas L., 1974, *The Historicity of the Patriarchal Narratives: the Quest for the Historical Abraham*

Trocmé, Etienne, 1997, *The Childhood of Christianity*

Vermes, Geza, 1973, *Jesus the Jew*

Vermes, Geza, 1993, *The Religion of Jesus the Jew*

Vermes, Geza, 2005, *The Passion*

Williams, Rowan, 2000, *Christ on Trial*

Yahuda, A.S., 1934, *The Accuracy of the Bible*

NOTES

1. Oddly enough, given the supposedly greater authority of science, the modern world has seen a considerable growth in so-called 'fundamentalist' readings of the Bible, most notably in the United States. These see scripture as 'inerrant' (incapable of error): 'We affirm that the Scriptures are the supreme written norm by which God binds the conscience, and that the authority of the Church is subordinate to that of Scripture. We deny that church creeds, councils, or declarations have authority greater than or equal to the authority of the Bible ... We affirm that Scripture in its entirety is inerrant, being free from all falsehood, fraud, or deceit. We deny that Biblical infallibility and inerrancy are limited to spiritual, religious, or redemptive themes, exclusive of assertions in the fields of history and science. We further deny that scientific hypotheses about earth history may properly be used to overturn the teaching of Scripture on creation and the flood.' (Chicago Statement on Biblical Inerrancy, 1978)

2. See for example Thomas L. Thompson, *The Historicity of the Patriarchal Narratives: The Quest for the Historical Abraham*, 1974.

3. Robin Lane Fox, *The Unauthorised Version: Truth and Fiction in the Bible*, 1991, p. 229.

4. Shlomo Sand, *The Invention of the Jewish People*, 2009, p. 121.

5. Lane Fox, op. cit., p. 237.

6. Quotations are as follows: 1: Ezekiel 5:8–10; 2: Deuteronomy 28:47–57; 3: Leviticus 25:45–46; 4: Deuteronomy 21:18–21;

5: Ecclesiastes 3:19; 6: Psalm 137:8–9; 7: Proverbs 17:8 and 21:14–15; 8: Joshua 10:39–40; 9: Genesis 9:2; and 10: Sura 110 of the Qur'an.

7. John Barton and John Muddiman, *The Oxford Bible Commentary*, 2001, p. 7.

8. The argument of this passage closely follows Richard Elliott Friedman's *Who Wrote the Bible?*, 1998.

9. For a dissenting view, see Paula Fredriksen, *From Jesus to Christ*, 2000, pp. xix–xx.

10. Ibid., p. 18.

11. See also 1 Corinthians 7:31, 1 Thessalonians 5:2, 2 Thessalonians 1:6–10, 2 Timothy 3:1, Hebrews 9:26 and 10:25 and 37, James 5:8, 2 Peter 3:10–12, 1 John 2:18, Jude 1:18.

12. Reza Aslan, *Zealot: The Life and Times of Jesus of Nazareth*, 2013, p. 31. Used by permission of Penguin Random House LLC.

13. Paul Q. Beeching, *Awkward Reverence: Reading the New Testament Today*, Bloomsbury Continuum, 1997, pp. 7, 15. © Paul Beeching, used by permission of Bloomsbury Publishing Inc.

14. Aslan, op. cit., p. 31.

15. See Lane Fox, op. cit., pp. 28–33.

16. David Dewey, *Which Bible? A Guide to English Translations*, 2004, p. 174.

17. Beeching, op. cit., p. 5.

18. Aslan, op. cit., p. 166.

19. Beeching, op. cit., p. 15, emphasis added.

20. Aslan, op. cit., p. 165.

21. E.P. Sanders, *Jesus and Judaism*, 1985, cited in Lane Fox, op. cit., p. 285.

22. See Geza Vermes, *The Passion*, 2005, pp. 20–24 for an exhaustive demonstration that such a meeting would have been completely out of the question.

23. Ibid., p. 111.

24. Paula Fredriksen, *Jesus of Nazareth, King of the Jews*, 2000, p. 223; see also Vermes, op. cit., 2005, p. 102.

25. For a fascinating and very plausible account of the reasons behind this, see Lane Fox, op. cit., p. 300.

26. Aslan, op. cit., p. 156.

27. Paula Fredriksen, *From Jesus to Christ* (2nd edn), 2000, p. 55.

28. Aslan, op. cit., pp. 183–4.

29. Lane Fox, op. cit., p. 285.

30. Cited in Aslan, op. cit., p. 53.

31. Cited in ibid., p. 242.

32. Cited in Fredriksen, *From Jesus to Christ*, p. 213.

33. Fredriksen, ibid., p. 212.

34. Beeching, op. cit., p. 4.

35. Fredriksen, *From Jesus to Christ*, p 180.

36. Though see Etienne Trocmé, *The Childhood of Christianity*, 1997, p. 37, for a very plausible alternative view.

37. Fredriksen, *From Jesus to Christ*, p. 185.

38. Fredriksen, ibid., p. 192.

39. Fredriksen, ibid., p. 199.

40. Much of the dualism of John is also found in the Dead Sea Scrolls: see J.H. Charlesworth, 'A Critical Comparison of the Dualism in 1QS 3:13–4:26 and the "Dualism" Contained

in the Gospel of John', in *John and the Dead Sea Scrolls*, ed. J.H. Charlesworth (New York: Crossroad, 1990).

41. Lane Fox, op. cit., p. 300.

42. H. Northrop Frye, *The Secular Scripture: A Study of the Structure of Romance*, 1976, p. 13 and passim.

43. Beeching, op. cit., pp. 15, 18.

44. Geza Vermes, *Jesus the Jew*, 1973, pp. 53–60.

45. A Cynic philosopher (F. Gerald Downing, *Christ and the Cynics: Jesus and Other Radical Preachers in First-Century Tradition*, 1988); a Jewish sage (Ben Witherington III, *Jesus the Sage: the Pilgrimage of Wisdom*, 1994); a political agitator and rebel with an agenda of social justice (John Dominic Crossan, *Jesus: A Revolutionary Biography*, 1994, and Richard A. Horsley, *Jesus and the Spiral of Violence: Popular Jewish Resistance in Roman Palestine,* 1987); and a passionate prophet of the approaching End Time (Paula Fredriksen, *From Jesus to Christ* (2nd edition) and *Jesus of Nazareth, King of the Jews*, both 2000, Marcus Borg, *Jesus: A New Vision*, 1988, E.P. Sanders, *Jesus and Judaism*, 1985, John P. Meier, *A Marginal Jew: Rethinking the Historical Jesus*, Vol. 1, 1991, and Vol. 2, 1994, and N.T. Wright, *Who Was Jesus?*, 1992).

46. In this context we must not forget the remarkable Julius Wellhausen, who, not content with revolutionising Old Testament scholarship, remarked later in his life that *'Jesus war kein Christ, sondern Jude'* – 'Jesus was not a Christian, but a Jew' (Wellhausen, 1905, cited in Markus Bockmuehl, *Seeing the Word: Refocusing New Testament Study*, 2006, p. 201).

47. Aslan, op. cit., p. 101.

48. Rowan Williams, *Christ on Trial*, 2000, p. 76.

49. Aslan, op. cit., p. 111.

50. Fredriksen, *Jesus of Nazareth, King of the Jews*, p. 210.

51. Fredriksen, ibid., pp. 247, 252.

52. Theodor Mommsen, cited in Sand, op. cit., p. 154.

53. Erich Auerbach, *Mimesis: The Representation of Reality in Western Literature*, 1953, p. 45.

54. Ibid., p. 555.

55. The argument of this latter part of the chapter draws heavily on H. Northrop Frye's *The Great Code: The Bible and Literature*, 1981.

56. H. Northrop Frye, *The Anatomy of Criticism*, 1957, p. 315.

57. Ibid., p. 56.

58. Frye, *The Great Code: The Bible and Literature*, pp. 41, 48. Used by permission of Victoria University in the University of Toronto.

59. Ibid., p. 171.

60. Ibid., pp. 219–20.

61. Ibid., p. 212.

62. Ibid., p. 232.

INDEX

Books of the Bible

THE BIBLE FOR GROWN-UPS

Main index

camels 24–5

Catholicism, Roman 3, 4, 6, 7, 22, 36, 38–9, 122

Christian missionaries (1st century AD) 118–21, 136, 138–9, 146, 201–03

Christianity 5–6, 27, 29, 33, 36, 38, 75, 97, 109, 112–19, 135, 144, 198, 203, 256

Christians, early 83–9, 114, 125, 133, 141, 149, 156, 166–7, 171, 173, 177–8, 199, 200

Clarke, John 180

contraception 6, 36

Covenant Code 64

Creation story 40–50, 55, 57, 60, 87

Crucifixion 7, 99–101, 103, 106–08, 128, 137, 141, 146–7, 160–2, 172, 182, 185, 192, 194, 229, 230, 242, 246

D

D (Deuteronomist) Bible author 15, 40, 55–8, 60

David, King 12, 20, 24, 27–9, 51, 70, 151, 184, 212–18, 234

ancestor of Jesus 93–5, 211, 247

David and Bathsheba 29, 72, 211–19

marries non-Israelite 36

'son of God' 129

Dead Sea Scrolls 80

Diaspora 61, 84, 114–15, 136, 139, 150, 165–8, 170

disciples 88, 91, 103, 106, 117, 141, 145–7, 160, 183, 199, 203

after the death of Jesus 84, 144, 153–4

divorce 6

E

E (Elohist) Bible author 14, 40, 54, 56–7, 60, 262

Ebionites 134

Eden, Garden of 23, 46–8, 54, 211, 246

Egypt 9–11, 17, 18, 23–5, 35, 96

as metaphor 245–7, 256

see also Bible, parallels between Old and New Testament

Ehrenzweig, Anton 238

El/Elohim 39–40, 54

Elijah 71, 184, 198–9, 247, 253

Elisha 184

Epistles 4, 85, 87, 99, 110–11, 137, 143, 178, 199, 210, 228, 240

Essenes 80

evangelists 89, 90, 92, 99–102, 109, 140, 149, 247

Exodus/exodus 23–7, 29, 235, 241, 253

Ezekiel 71

F

Flood, the 28, 55, 57, 60

INDEX

Joseph of Arimathea 80
Josephus 79, 107, 131, 134, 202
Judah/Judea 10, 12, 17, 18, 51, 52, 60, 69, 78–9, 81–2, 130–3
Judas 174

K
Kingdom of God 111, 130, 153, 164, 187, 193, 245

L
Lane Fox, Robin 103, 271–4
Last Supper 103–4, 105, 111, 128, 174, 230
Levites 64, 68
Lot 34–5
Luke 88, 90, 116, 141, 148–68, 220–30, 237
Luther, Martin 6, 185

M
Mark 88, 95, 111, 141, 144–8, 149–51, 169, 187, 198, 230–35
see also messianic secret
Mary (mother of Jesus) 7, 94, 96–7, 135, 160, 208, 222–5, 228–9
perpetual virginity 7
Mary and Martha 126, 158
Matthew 88, 91–2, 93–8, 141, 148–9, 151–6, 228
McGrath, Alister 255

messiah 95, 97, 99–101, 138, 141, 145, 184–9, 196–7, 245
messianic secret 141, 145, 187–8, 196
miracles 99, 183–5, 187, 191, 193
Mommsen, Theodor 202
Moses 20, 25, 38–9, 54, 61–3, 100, 102, 220, 221, 236, 254
and myth 221
competition with Aaron 52, 55, 57–8
forerunner of Jesus 83, 96, 102, 152, 184, 243–4, 247
importance in Christianity 198
myth and metaphor 238–48

N
Nathan 71, 199, 211, 215, 217–19, 234, 254
Nativity 158, 220–30
Nazareth 81, 94–6, 127, 223
New Testament 3, 4, 6, 8, 17, 77–203, 221, 232, 238–48, 254, 265–6
as history 89–109, 111, 130–9, 144–8
canon 139, 176–9
morality and values 120–30
structure 83–9
when written 143
who wrote 139–80
writings not included 177, 179

• 283 •